WITHDRAWN

FILTH
ART OF CLOCKWORK APPLIQUE
84147410

D1461121

THE ART OF CUTWORK AND APPLIQUÉ
Historic, Modern and Kuna Indian

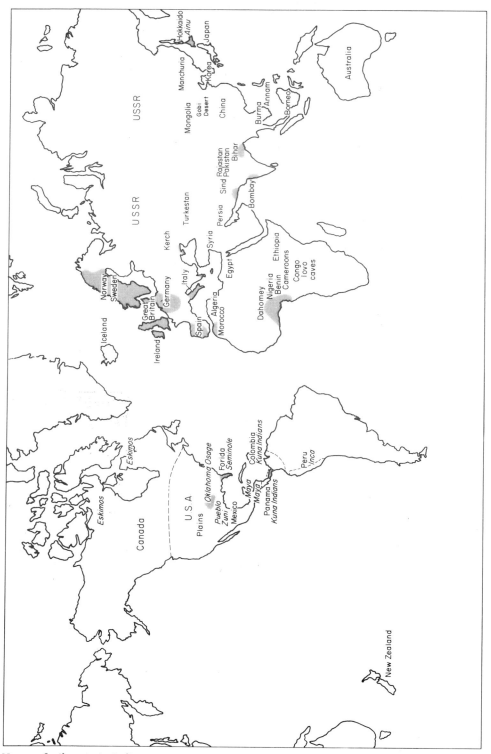

Names of tribes are in *italics*
Work described in the text comes from areas shown shaded on the map

The Art of Cutwork and Appliqué

HISTORIC, MODERN AND KUNA INDIAN

Herta Puls

CHESTER COLLEGE

ACC. No.   DEPT. b

841474

CLASS No.

746.44b PUL

LIBRARY

BT BATSFORD LTD · LONDON

To Oky

© Herta Puls 1978

First published 1978
ISBN 0 7134 0476 0

Filmset in 'Monophoto' Apollo by
Servis Filmsetting Limited, Manchester
Printed in Great Britain by
The Anchor Press Ltd Tiptree Essex
for the publishers
B.T. Batsford Limited
4 Fitzhardinge Street
London W1H 0AH

Contents

Acknowledgment   6

Introduction   7

Symbols and their use   11

Cutwork   29

Appliqué   77

The Kuna Indians and their Mola embroidery   117

Working methods for Kuna Indian appliqué   153

   Kuna molas selected for their artistic merit   180

A personal approach   203

Technical information   234

Bibliography   237

Index   239

Acknowledgment

My grateful thanks to Constance Howard, without whose encouragement and support this book would not have been written, and to my husband who accompanied me on the research trips and acted as photographer, travel agent, critic and patient listener.

I would also like to thank all my friends who have helped with the research for my book by sending me information from many parts of the world, especially Dr med. Liselotte Brauns in Germany and Mrs Ann W. Davis in the USA; Carol Eiss from the USA for sending me my first mola; Dr med. M.C. Waechter for providing valuable cutwork samples; the Torell family for putting up my husband and me during our research in Sweden; Anne Wenzel in Panama City for guidance and advice on mola buying; John Mann of the San Blas Islands for his most instructive mola talk; Mr Jonathan Leonard of the Pan-American Health organisation for introducing me to the Kuna Indian Baptist missionary Peter Miller and his wife Clementina on the island of Ailigandi; Peter and Clementina Miller for their warm welcome and hospitality, without whose knowledge and advice we would not have seen or learned the customs and life of their people.

I also gratefully acknowledge The British Museum, Miss Bateman and Mr Picton; the Ethnographic Museum in Gothenburg, Mrs Rose-Marie Cooper, and the Völkerkunde Museum in Hamburg, Prof Zwernemann and Dr W. Haberland; the Altonaer Museum in Hamburg, Frau Gisela Soltkahn; the Textile Museum in Krefeld, Frau Dr Brigitte Menzel, all of whom opened their archives and did everything to help us in our research; and the members of the '62 Group who allowed me to use photographs of their work.

Thanks too to Frau Thekla Gombert and Dietmar Carsten in Germany and Joss Graham in London who made available their beautiful collections of cutwork, Kuna Indian artifacts and Indian textiles respectively, and Jeanette Durrant for letting me use her African photographs.

Also my thanks to Mr C.J. Webb of the London School of Hygiene and Tropical Medicine for so expertly dealing with the incessant demands for copies and prints of photographs and slides and to Derek Stafford who organised the photographic material and the lay-out of the book.

London 1978   HP

Introduction

Before describing the ancient crafts of Cutwork and Appliqué and the special decorative way in which the Kuna Indian women of Panama use them in their dress, it is important to look at embroidery in general and to remember that it is not a separate entity. From the time of early man it was used on garments for practical purposes, mainly for protection from the elements. It then began to play a vital part in the visual expression of religion and mythology and the identification of status in the community, it helped with visual communication, and finally it was used purely as decoration.

The lavishly embroidered gowns and finely woven, knitted and embellished textiles in which people, from the beginning of recorded time, buried their dead cannot have been meaningless artifacts or pure decoration, just as the symbolic paintings and writing on walls of graves and coffins were not without significance. Many of these relics of ancient culture were discovered hidden in deep caves and burial mounds which, once closed, were not intended to be seen again by a living person. They were evidence of a strong belief in the continuation of an existence after death. These symbols, embroidered or written, were communications between the supernatural world and the soul of the deceased before it reached its final resting place.

Our highly industrialised and sophisticated society tends to make us value embroidery only as decoration, although we still make use of symbolism on regalia and ceremonial garments, church banners and school blazers for identification. Even our present generation with its uniform of denim jeans and its aim of sex equality is feeling the need for personal and group identification. By embroidering symbols such as flowers and initials on these garments they have found a way of expressing their individuality and their belonging to a group.

We often use the craft as a leisure activity, which gives us the aesthetic pleasure of working with fabrics, threads and colour. We can find proof in our own Western history and in ancient civilisations that there is much more to the embellishment of fabrics and clothes than mere aesthetic pleasure.

From the necessity of joining skins or pelts with leather strips and sewing woven or knitted fabrics together for protection against inclement weather, nomadic man developed the skill of expressing spiritual values on articles used for religious ceremonies and for his own general use. He progressed through the centuries to a very high aesthetic standard of the work which he created, motivated by his spiritual beliefs and always governed by the nature of the materials he used. In settled communities with more time and materials available for these pursuits, the ornamentation became more elaborate, richer materials were being used and the symbolism expressed not only religious fervour and belief but combined it with practical use, executed by both men and women, amateurs and professionals.

We know that 2300 years before Christ decoration on dress denoted rank among the Syrians and Phoenicians. The Assyrians and Babylonians wore girdles trimmed with tassels and garments embroidered according to the dignity of the wearer. Status was indicated by the amount of trimming on the full-length skirt and the colour of the decoration. It also differentiated between priests and royalty. In the fourth and fifth centuries BC the priests in Media and Persia were clothed in white when performing their official duties, only they wore a sacred girdle. The cut of their garments varied with their rank. Victorious Roman generals wore the *tunica palmata* at their victory ceremonies which was embroidered in gold with palm branches. Two purple stripes, *clavi*, varying in width indicated the rank and calling of the wearer. These were attached to the front and back of the Roman toga and tunica. The servant classes of thirteenth-century Germany often wore garments made from several pieces of different fabrics and colours. These were those of the coat of arms of their mistresses. At the end of the century, the women who had a right to coats of arms used the colours for their own dresses and also embroidered them with the armorial bearings in hemmed or couched appliqué. Through the centuries the type of dress and richness of costume worn by the aristocracy, the priests and upper classes, were copied by the ordinary people, unless it was forbidden by law to wear the fineries and status symbols of these classes. In China, a full range of embroidered symbols was reserved for the exclusive use by the emperor. The aristocracy also used embroidery on horse-trappings and banners for identification in battle and at court. The symbols, often animals or objects, were simplified and stylised for easy recognition and developed into heraldry. Richly decorated church vestments and linens, beautifully embroidered with Christian symbols and pictorial representations of biblical stories and scenes from the life of Christ in the *Opus Anglicanum* period of the thirteenth to fourteenth centuries in England (1250–1350), expressed not only deep religious feeling but were means of communication between the priests and their largely illiterate congregation. Another example of embroidery which communicated by telling the story of the Norman Conquest in a delightful lively pictorial way in AD 1077, is the Bayeux Tapestry, a hanging of 230 feet (70 metres) in length.

When embroidery was used for secular purposes the symbolism became pure decoration and fashion. After the dissolution of the monastries even church embroidery was cut up for other uses. When wealth increased and the ornamentation became more exuberant, one of the great dangers was that the symbols ceased to have any meaning and became just beautiful embellishment. When the craft became neglected because of continuous copying with alien threads and colours on unsuitable materials without spiritual motivation, decline set in.

I find it astonishing that a revival of interest in the craft often goes hand in hand with special attention to the techniques but without thought of design. The result is the exaggerated importance which is given to the execution. This inhibits free design and invention and makes it akin to the designs and techniques of the industrial machine. Could it be that the materialistic society of Western civilisation has no strong spiritual beliefs and values on which to base their designs and little motivation to inspire them to express these?

Research into the fascinating history of textiles with its many different developments will continue. No writing about it can ever be complete. During the research new aspects become apparent all the time. Even an extensive collection of photographs cannot present a complete picture. I have tried to make the reader aware of the wide-reaching influence of embroidery into every aspect of life. I hope that I have stimulated a desire to investigate all the many features which I had to omit.

Ivory king wearing a crown of Upper
Egypt. First dynasty, 3400 BC
Drawing by Derek Stafford

10

Symbols and their use

Cutwork and appliqué designs of the Kuna Indian Molas developed in a comparatively short time from religious symbols painted on body and cloth to picturing objects from their environment and finally to story telling. This development took place within the limits of a complicated textile or embroidery technique which is unique. How advanced their culture was before the Spaniards came is still a mystery, but more remains to be discovered in the as yet unexplored Kuna territory of Panama.

In the rest of the world the same initial start of cutting and applying a piece of cloth for probably the same purpose of conveying ideas through symbols, practised over many centuries, has produced very different results.

Many of the designs which we find on ancient textiles and sculpture appear in slightly modified form all over the world and through the centuries. Some symbols taken from nature and the environment were stylised to such an extent that they became geometric shapes. They were often distributed by traders but were also created simultaneously in different parts of the world.

When the trackers and hunters began to settle and their mode of life changed to farming, success was dependent on observation of nature. They began to relate the rising and setting of sun and moon and the movement of the stars to the changes from night to day and, most important, to the changing of the seasons. The sun, the life giving rains and the winds in the changing seasons were essential for the growing of the crops to the first agriculturists.

It seems a logical step that they should record these observations by symbols and that they should have created the symbol of the cross, which is perhaps the most ancient of all. The discovery of north and south and their relation to east and west brought into existence the equal limbed cross symbol, representing the four cardinal points. The great importance of this discovery led to the belief of supernatural powers or gods connected with these points. They believed in a power which emanated from a fixed point, the Pole star, which was responsible for the circulating of the heavenly bodies and the recurring seasons. Many variations of the cross developed, one of the oldest and most widespread form found is the swastika. In a twelfth century manuscript in the British Museum (*Anonymi Commentarius in Apocalypsin Add*. 11, 695) the revolving swastika symbol is shown among the star symbols in a celestial wheel. This form of the cross, a religious or religious/magic good-luck symbol according to its ancient sanscrit name, is of considerable antiquity. It was found early in Asia Minor, Central,

Western and Northern Europe, India, where it was a favoured Buddhist symbol, China and Japan and in pre-Columbian America. In Egypt it was not found until a few years before the Christian era. It was a sacred pagan symbol, which was adopted with other pre-Christian symbols by the early Christians and used freely in the catacombs in Rome. According to the position of the arms added to the limbs of the cross, good or evil is believed to emanate from this sign.

In the search for the explanation of the mysteries of life, especially the beginning of all life, man found the perfect symbol in the spiral. Its shape was visible in nature in whirlpools and whirlwinds, on shells, the coiled serpents and the spiral growth of many plants. The spiral growth in nature represented a life giving power. Many examples of its use in ancient times exist, it is a symbol of great importance in many cultures. The spiral became the birth symbol, indicating the movement of the child at birth. Whorled shells were used as amulets outside bedrooms to assist birth in Hindu countries and a red spiral was reported to have been found painted on Hindu bedroom doors, when a birth was about to take place. In pre-Columbian Mexico it was believed that the moon presided over human generations and its sign was always placed by the sign of the sun. A sea snail was pictured with these to denote that man came from his mother's womb as the snail creeps from its shell. The spiral shape of the healed navel did not escape observation. The importance of the connection between the navel string, afterbirth and creation shows in the customs which were observed during their disposal. Great importance is attached to the umbilical cord in the Kuna mythology and picture-writing. Instead of using the spiral symbol they depict the navel string as a zigzag line. This line of triangles is also a strong design feature in their mola embroidery. Triangles pointing down have been used to describe female and pointing up male sexuality as well as fertility and have been found in prehistoric caves scratched on rocks and are used by North American Indians in their drawings and in their beadwork.

The power which was responsible for creating the whirlwinds and whirlpools, which also seemed to start from a centre, was believed to be supernatural and led to the belief in celestial whirlpools. Whirlwinds were believed to carry supernatural beings, or the souls of the dead to the heavens. In the Ethiopic book of Enoch reference is made to the four winds which bear up the earth and the firmament of the heavens, constituting the pillars of heaven. The Egyptians depicted the god who supports the heavens sometimes with the Y symbol, the sky pillars, repeated four times. This Y-shaped symbol is often used on Kuna Indian molas and when I asked for an explanation, I was told that it was the shape of the stick which they use to lift their clothes up to the highest wooden joist in their huts. Any more or older significance of this frequently occurring symbol was not known.

Rains, which made the crops grow and created the whirlpools, came from heaven and the spiral shape of the coiled serpent became the symbol for the rain god who brought the life-saving water.

It is hardly surprising that these two symbols, the cross with all its variations and the spiral, singly or in combination, can be found worldwide and that evidence for this exists from earliest records.

These symbols together with others (developed, for instance, from trees and the shell of the ear) were the elements of picture-writing in the Egyptian and Arabic languages and also in the writing of the Kuna language. The picture-writing of the Kuna Indians may have developed as a result of European influence. Just as the ancient Peruvians had no written language, it is believed that the Kunas communicated only with the spoken word.

Graphic symbols were also used as identification marks, for self-glorification and for the protection from evil forces. They were repeated as patterns and executed in painting, textile printing, embroidery, metal and carved in wood and stone. From simple bold designs, which could be recognised from a distance, work grew, which had elaborate detail on finer materials. This same development can be observed in the changing styles of architecture. Man's life style and culture is reflected in the buildings he creates, the clothes he wears and in the artifacts which he designs to express his philosophy. Each is related to the other in any one period. In the few isolated communities which are still living in the uncomplicated life style of centuries ago, the relationship between these symbols and their deep religious beliefs is still very strong, even when the significance of each detail of the design is not known.

One of the most common features on the dress of gods, priests and royalties in paintings, on metal, wood or stone sculpture from pre-Christian times is the use of fringes and tassels as a status symbol. We find it in Europe, Asia, Africa and America and they are easily recognised. Cutwork and appliqué, which are special techniques of a textile craft, although found in every country, are more difficult to identify with certainty. Very old textiles are rare and this presents the problem of recognising the type of fabric and technique used on objects which picture textiles. A great deal of interpretation is therefore based on guesswork but one thing is certain, as far back as we have evidence, the imagination and skill of the people who were working with textiles has been superb and highly accomplished throughout the centuries.

As our interest in historical textiles grows and our methods in dealing with the excavations and reclaiming of ancient 'lost sites' improves, more items will be discovered and preserved. This should help us to fill some of the gaps in our knowledge of the important part textiles played in the past.

In the meantime the evidence available on other materials, such as stone, metal and wood, and reports written by people who lived in those times will have to be taken into consideration to complete the picture.

Drawing from Demon Stone, San
Augustin Culture. Probably AD 1000 San
Augustin, Colombia. Height (76·5 cm)
31½ in. Abstracted faces become
inspiration for masks

Kuna Indian Molas with mask design,
worked in three layers of coloured cotton.
Panel 45·7 cm × 68·6 cm (18 in. × 27 in.)
Detail showing the use of patterned fabric
for patches
British Museum, London

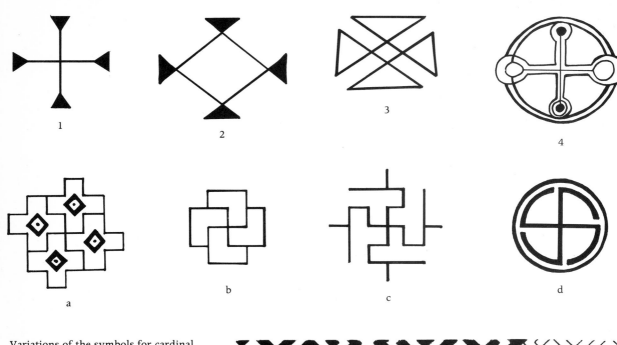

Variations of the symbols for cardinal
points. Stone-age cave drawings from
Lovo, Congo. (1–3)
Sun enclosing cardinal points, Lovo,
Congo (4)
Adaptation of the swastika symbol.
(a) Four godhouses. Zuni – Red Indians
(b) Japan, (c) Annam, (d) Swastika turning
in the syn symbol with openings for the
winds to enter

Basket from the San Blas Islands, Panama

(a) Fret pattern (b–c) fret and cross symbols used in stone work on the walls of buildings at Mitla Oaxaca, Mexico, c.AD 1000

Lectern fall at the Baptist mission house
on Ailigandi, San Blas, worked by the
Kuna Indians in three layers of cotton
fabric in their appliqué technique, using
the cross and variations of the Y symbol

a

b

c

(a) symbol of sea shell from the temple of
Quetzalcoatl in Teotihuacana, Mexico,
(b) Spiral symbols on the walls of
buildings at Mitla Oaxaca, Mexico,
(c) Drawing of spiral movement in sea
shell

Toltec Wall of Serpents, from Coatipanti
c.AD 1000
Anthropological Museum, Mexico City

Beaded legband using cross symbol. Kuna
Indians, San Blas, Panama

Kuna Indian Mola with adaptation of Y-symbol

Ethnographic Museum, Gothenburg, Sweden (a)

Nakkrus or Nas Nasi, a pre-Christian cross, used by the Kuna Indians to exorcise evil spirits. The stick in the crotch is spun up and over the roof (b) Arrangement of Y-symbols (c) This geometric pattern can be repeated in any direction. It is a very adaptable design for a garment, as it can be used for any size required

a

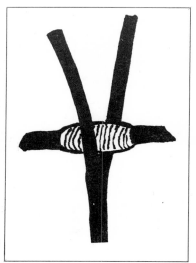

b

c

23

Mexican figure in baked clay 31·8 cm
(12½ in.) high, *c.*AD 500–1000. Dress
shows fertility and cross symbols

Maya sculpture. Dress, jewellery and
hairstyle were all signs of status. The
incised decoration on the blouse or huipil
differs from presentation of a printed
fabric and must have been quilted or
embroidered
Anthropological Museum, Mexico City

Pre-Columbian pottery figure from the
Valley of Mexico wearing a fringed skirt
with relief pattern
British Museum, London
Figure on a ceremonial lime stone vessel
at Ebla in Syria 1900 BC. The ceremonial
garment has a fringe edging

Decoration of an animal–demon warrior
on a baked clay jug from Peru. Height
20·3 cm (8 in.). The dress is fringed and
has surface decoration which could be
printed or embroidered

Cutwork

To the traditional embroiderer the term *cutwork* is divided into clearly defined stages of decorating a textile, usually linen or cotton, with designs which are left by cutting away fabric or threads and filling the resulting spaces with more or less elaborate stitchery. *Simple cutwork*, *Renaissance embroidery*, *Richelieu work*, *Venetian cutwork* and *Italian cutwork* are all well known terms used to describe a progressively more and more lacelike fabric. In the wider sense both *broderie Anglaise* and the pinked and slashed style of costume of the fifteenth century in France, which was adopted in England, are cutwork techniques. Even simple button-holes or neck openings are 'cuts' which are either left raw, have a bound edge, or are embellished.

Cutwork and appliqué are two directly opposed but nevertheless closely related techniques of sewing and embroidery. The fabrics or threads, which are cut away in one place, can be put onto or applied in another. The application of threads is called *couching*, a method used with precious metal threads, but also for applying threads and cords to the edges of fabric shapes which have been stitched or applied to a background.

When man fastened together pieces of skin or cloth and repaired damaged articles, cutwork and appliqué must have been the two methods used, not only for making and mending everyday articles of apparel but also for decoration. The stitches they used they had learned from their experience with manipulating grasses and plant fibres for baskets. Whipping developed into overcast, looped and buttonhole stitches; intertwining led to weaving. The very nature of textiles makes it difficult to find direct evidence of how early man made and used textiles. Wear, light, dirt, damp, heat and bugs break down fibres and our evidence must often be taken from more durable materials, such as metal or stone sculpture, paintings and written reports which have survived the centuries.

From the extant material available, I have collected and photographed samples which show the simple stages of cutwork to the most delicate and elaborate *durchbruch* samples worked in Germany, from as many countries as I could find, using 'cutwork' in the widest sense of the term.

The first appearance of fine lacelike cutwork cannot be given with certainty. Lace as such is mentioned in royal accounts in 1492. In the twelfth century linen embroidery became established in Germany and northern countries of Europe. Flax, which was grown in these parts, was cheaper than silk, gold and silver threads. It was worked predominently on vestments in convents by nuns but it also was used for domestic items. These wore out through hard use and no examples have remained. Many of the church and altar furnishings were made of linen and some exquisitely worked examples still exist. The convent of Lüne near Lüneburg in Germany, a medieval Hanseatic town on the ancient salt road, has a remarkable collection, especially Lenten cloths (Hungertücher). These are kept in air-conditioned rooms because of their fineness and frailty, also because of their great rarity and the cost of protection. They are only exhibited for one week in August each year. On this occasion the army is called out to guard them. After the Reformation the monastries and convents were suppressed and many nuns went back to their home areas, where they taught the craft they had learned to local girls and women. The designs on linen were created by openwork grounds, either by drawn thread or pulled work, contrasted by raised and many surface stitches, such as buttonhole, darning, chain and knot stitches. These embroideries may have been the forerunners of the Italian and Spanish linen embroidery of later date. Many ways for achieving openwork embroideries were developed, especially in Italy. *Punto tagliato* (cutwork) progressed through various stages to finally *punto in aria* (needlepoint lace), *punto* meaning stitch. *Point de Saxe*, or Dresden work, was quilting combined with surface stitchery and outlining, worked through two layers of linen, one fine layer and a coarse backing. The coarse layer was cut away in those places which had first been outlined and fine open work, either pulled or drawn thread, was worked in the space on the remaining fine linen. In Italy drawn thread work was called *punto tirato*.

The net background for *lacis* or *guipure d'art* or *filet* could be made either by knotting or, on linen gauze, by creating the holes either by pulled work or by drawing and cutting some warp and weft threads and overcasting the remaining threads. Features could then be darned into the created net or lacis background.

Gauze net could also be woven by using a twined stitch and the design darned into this netlike fabric. The earliest examples of this type of weave were found by Sir M Aurel Stein in Turkestan and attributed to China. The technique of weaving gauze by twisting two warp threads before working the next weft thread was probably also first used in early basketry. The Indians of ancient Peru of the pre-Inca period between AD 900 and AD 1400 wove a gauze cloth with a twined thread and used wool for the darning. A variation could be accomplished by working the net background on gauze around a shape.

Designs for these and other forms of cutwork and net embroidery were published in 1589 by Frederico di Vinciolo in a book: *Les Singuliers et Nouveaux Pourtraicts du Seigneur F. de Venitien pour toutes sortes d'Ouvrages de Lingerie* and in *New Mödel Buch* (New Pattern Book) *Von allerhand sonderbaren schönen Mödeln von der jetzt gebreuchliche durchgeschnittenen Arbeit durch HV angeordnet,* Strassburg 1596. (A variety of singularly beautiful patterns of the now popular cutwork. Arranged by HV Strassburg 1596.) Richard

30

Shorleyker published a pattern book in England in 1624. *A Schoolhouse for the Needle* which includes: 'Here followeth certaine patternes of cut-works newly invented and never published before.' Rhodes or punchwork created a fabric with holes by using the four-sided pulled fabric stitch. The Bushonga tribes of West Africa produced drawn thread embroidery on raffia cloth about AD 1600.

The fine medieval linen embroidery, later Dresden work, was introduced into Scotland by Luigi Ruffini in 1782 as a cottage industry. It gave work to the poor of Ayrshire. In 1814 Mrs Jamieson, an agent for embroidery, copied fillings from a French christening robe and taught them to her workers, who worked them on Scottish muslin. In 1830 this embroidery became known as *Ayrshire Embroidery*.

Madeira open work was first seen in England in 1850 and from this developed *broderie Anglaise*. *Richelieu embroidery* was based on sixteenth century *Italian cutwork*; it often used bands and braids, and the connecting bars had picots added. In the northern countries of Denmark and Sweden fine linen embroidery was worked in the same way as in Germany, Italy and Spain. A typical version from Norway is *Hardanger embroidery* and *Hedebo embroidery* from Denmark. In Hungary cutwork on linen was combined with black surface stitchery in bullion knots on dresses, blouses and head-scarves.

In my search for examples of fine cutwork in Germany, I met Frau Thekla Gombert, a woman in her early seventies who had qualified as an art teacher and gained her Diploma in Art and Embroidery at St Gallen in Switzerland. She had taught embroidery in the country district of Hessen-Schwalm, where she had visited all the farms in the neighbourhood to discover old embroideries. She found many beautiful examples worked by nuns who had gone home after the Reformation had closed their convents. Because the farmers would not let her buy the original pieces, she photographed them, borrowed them and faithfully copied many, so that the craft should not die without being recorded. She was kind enough to let me photograph many pieces of her beautiful historical collection. Instead of being made for altar furnishings, they were worked to record family history on *Familien Tücher* (family cloths), but also for other domestic purposes.

Many examples of appliqué use a combination of the two techniques of cutting and applying to decorate ecclesiastical and secular articles. For after all, to apply you have to cut first.

Man's suit in yellow satin.
The fabric is slashed, paned
and trimmed with braid
*Victoria and Albert
Museum, London*

Man's cloak, doublet and
breeches. English 1625–30
*Victoria and Albert
Museum, London*

Sketches from paintings by Hans Holbein and old masters around 1526. The slashes which were first used on tightly fitting garments to give the wearer more room to move became decoration. Braid was used to embellish and neaten them. Differently coloured linings were exposed and pulled through the slashes on sleeves, doublets and breeches

Facing page
Baskets from San Blas showing different weaves and overcasting

Italian cuff. Silk damask with buttonholes, late fourteenth century. *Victoria and Albert Museum, London* Cuts for buttonholes were neatened by overcasting or buttonhole stitch. Stitches as well as weaves were first used in basket making

Page 36
Sampler of buttonholes worked in 1781 on linen *Altonaer Landesmuseum*

Page 37
Detail of buttonholes and surface embroidery stitches which include eyelet holes

Sampler of fabric darning. Worn or torn holes were repaired by filling the hole with darning, replacing various types of weaves. This can be done in self colour, or witk coloured patterns. *Author's collection.* Size of sampler 27·5 cm × 29 cm (11 in. × 11½ in.) Detail of darning three times actual size

Facing page
Enlargement of pattern darning replacing worn fabric

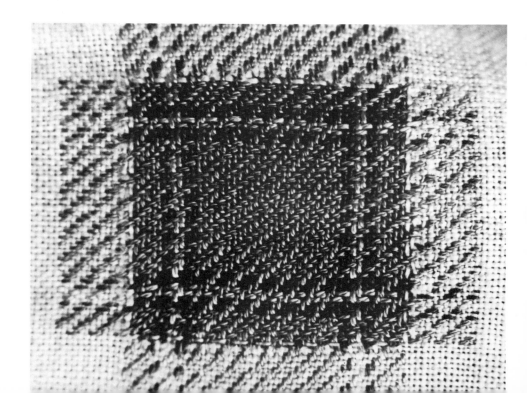

St Michael. Marble piece of pulpit,
Pisan 1275
Victoria and Albert Museum, London

Cutwork eyelet holes or broderie Anglaise
decoration seems to have been worked on
the sashes of the dress. The same
cutwork pattern is repeated on either
metal or wood portrayed by the casket
held by the angel. This dress decoration
cut into marble is more permanent than
the actual textile could ever be and bears
witness to the treatment of textiles in
bygone centuries

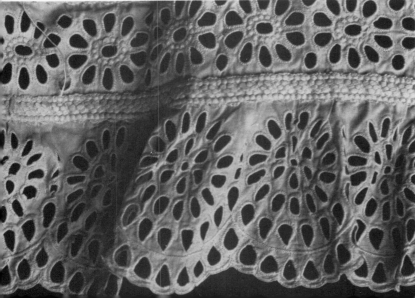

Child's dress. Nineteenth century with
detail of broderie Anglaise
Textile Museum, Krefeld-Germany

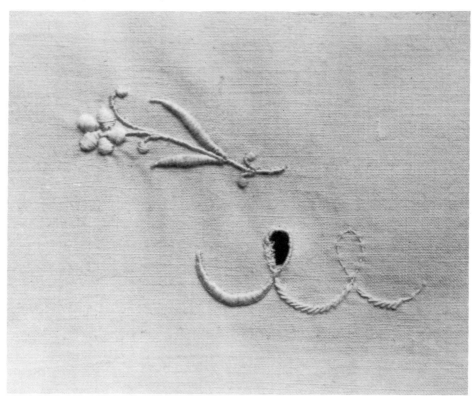

Cutwork working sampler. 1869. The size
of the piece of sampler shown is 17·8 cm
(7 in.) square. The scallops are outlined
with running and stemstitch, some are
overcast with blanket or buttonhole
stitch. The holes of the broderie Anglaise
are overcast
Author's collection
The enlarged small motive shows the
working process

Doyle worked in broderie Anglaise.
Nineteenth century.
Author's collection
Size 25·4 cm (10 in.) square

Facing page
Sampler of eyelet holes and surface
stitchery. Drawn thread and pulled
stitches also create holes. All stitches are
worked on linen with linen threads. Size
11 cm × 9·5 cm (4½ in. × 3¾ in.)
Altonaer Landesmuseum

Enlarged detail of sampler. The holes are
made by working blanket stitch into the
same place and pulling the threads of the
fabric to form a hole

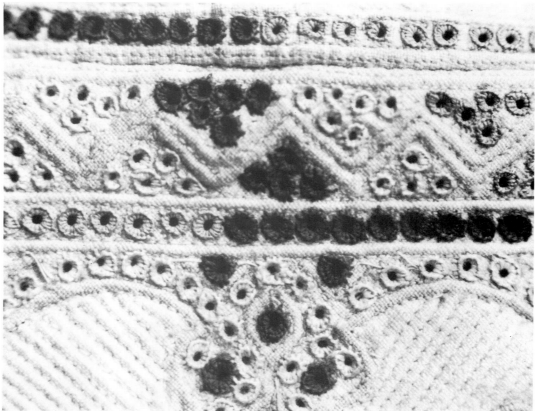

Nigerian cap worked with eyelet holes.
Nineteenth century. The detail shows
that the holes were achieved in the same
way as the sampler on page 45
Embroiderers' Guild collection

Tenth century fragment of ornamental
limestone, probably from the ruined
palace of Medina, Az-Zahra near Cordoba.
The Hispano-Arabic piece of sculpture
shows the affinity of cutwork in textiles
to sculptured decoration
Victoria and Albert Museum, London

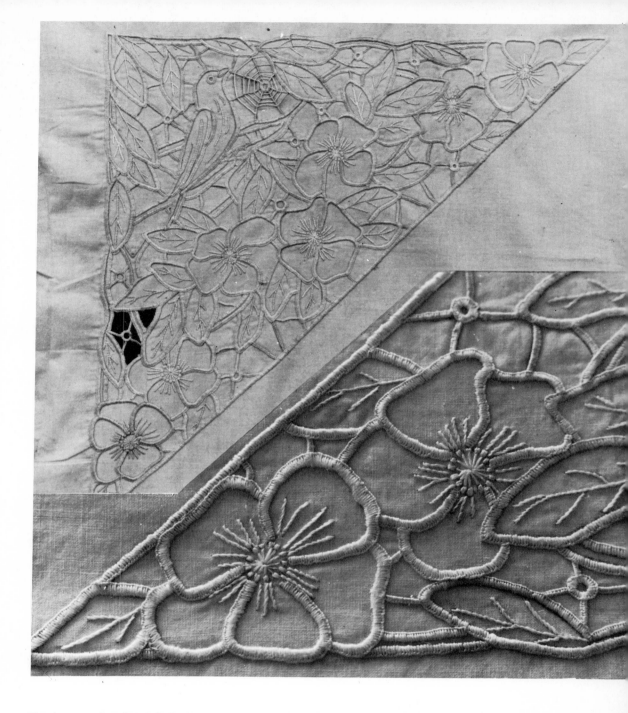

Simple cutwork. Fabric is linking all parts of the design. Worked by Mabel Duthie in buttonhole stitch with french knots, satin stitch and stemstitch on linen.
(a) Detail of a table mat in Renaissance embroidery. Bars have been added to link the shapes, these were worked in buttonhole or blanket stitch. The small holes were cut and overcast. Worked by Frau Behrens

Corner of a pillow case. c.1907 German.
Below: Detail of the corner before the fabric between the flowers and leaves and under the bars was cut and removed. Satin, stem stitch and french knots have been added

49

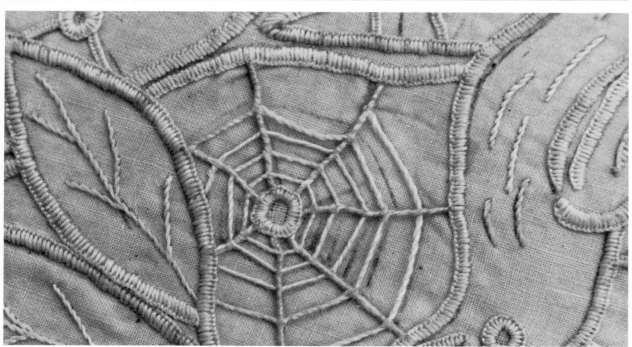

Facing page
Detail of the corner with Renaissance embroidery. Buttonholed bars had the material behind them cut away. Another detail of the same piece of work, showing finished bars and a spiderweb wheel. The bars of this have still to be worked in buttonhole stitch

Part of corner completely finished except for top right hand corner where fabric has to be cut from under the bars. Worked by Frau Behrens

Angel holding curtains in tufo stone.
Italian *circa* twelfth century
Victoria and Albert Museum, London

Sculpted dress embroidery. The
embroidery resembles eyelet holes, drawn
fabric work or punto in aria

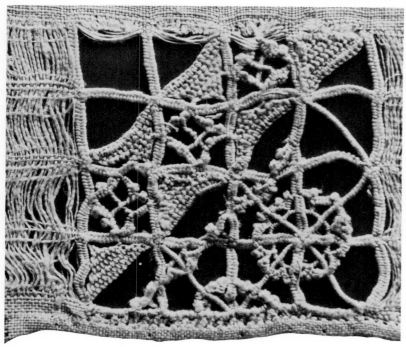

Mat from Italy. Punto in aria sixteenth century. Squares worked in buttonhole lace and needleweaving are contrasted by squares embroidered with drawn fabric stitches and satin stitch
Embroiderers' Guild collection

Detail of fragment of punto in aria. Warp and weft threads have been drawn and cut except for a small number. These remaining threads have been covered with buttonhole stitches or needleweaving. The spaces between the bars have been filled with needle lace worked in buttonhole stitch with picots. During the working of the embroidery the linen is tacked onto paper and the needle lace filling worked on the top of the paper, so avoiding distortion of the embroidery

Sampler of needle lace insertions, punto
in aria worked in 1772 on batiste
Altonaer Landesmuseum

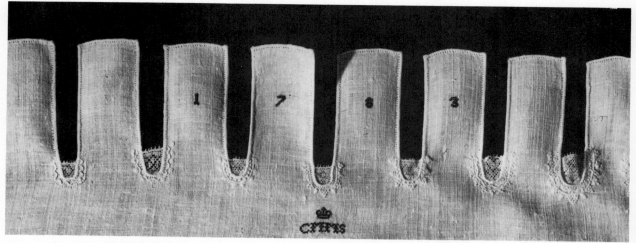

Sampler of shirt slits in needlepoint lace
and surface embroidery with eyelet holes,
chain stitch and knot stitch on linen
worked in 1783
Altonaer Landesmuseum

The Adoration of the Magi. Whale's bone, height 36·8 cm (14½ in.) *Victoria and Albert Museum, London* English, early twelfth century. This piece of ivory carving shows elaborate embroidery which could be quilting combined with cutwork and appliqué. Not many garments from these early centuries have survived and carvings like this show how accomplished was English embroidery of the eleventh and twelfth centuries

Ivory plaque. Panels of animals and birds
interlaced, probably Anglo-Saxon of the
eighth or ninth century. 14·5 cm × 8 cm
(6¼ in. × 3¼ in.)
Victoria and Albert Museum, London
The appearance and construction of the
ivory carving is similar to punto in aria

Hispano-Arabic ivory casket with metal
mounts from Cordoba shows great affinity
with needle lace, AD 975
Victoria and Albert Museum, London

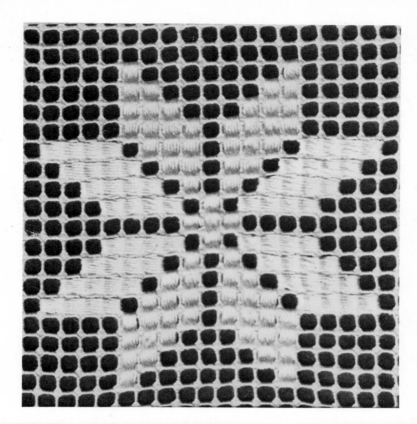

Facing page
Back section of a cap. Nürnberg, seventeenth century. This very fine piece of embroidery is worked by creating a net background with pulled fabric stitches around the shapes. Some of the shapes are filled with different drawn fabric stitches which create an almost lacelike effect
Textile Museum, Krefeld

A sampler of net background which was made by drawing threads and overcasting the remaining threads. The pattern was darned in afterwards
Frau Thekla Gombert

Detail of the back of cap (p58) showing the solid linen shapes and the various stitches used to work the lacelike fillings

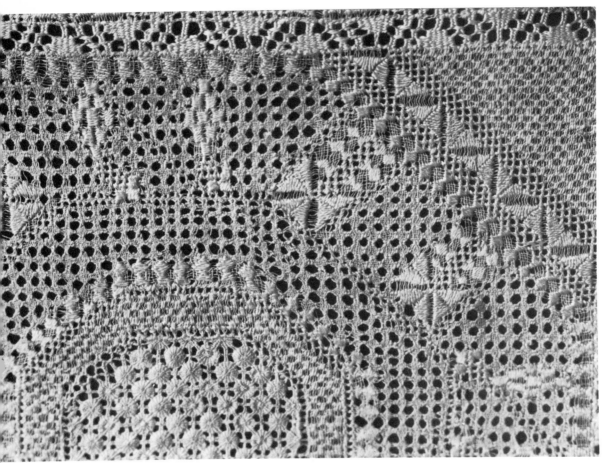

A piece of pulled or drawn fabric stitches
worked on fine linen. It shows a
combination of needleweaving, pulled
satin stitch, foursided stitch and wheel
fillings
Textile Museum, Krefeld

Facing page
Fragment of Italian cutwork, c.1600. The
design is first layed out with faggot
stitch. This can be seen on one side of the
sampler. Counted satin stitch is worked
next, then the cutwork. The buttonhole
stitch filling is worked without piercing
the ground fabric, except around the
edge. Finally the ground fabric is cut
away from behind the filling
Embroiderers' Guild Collection

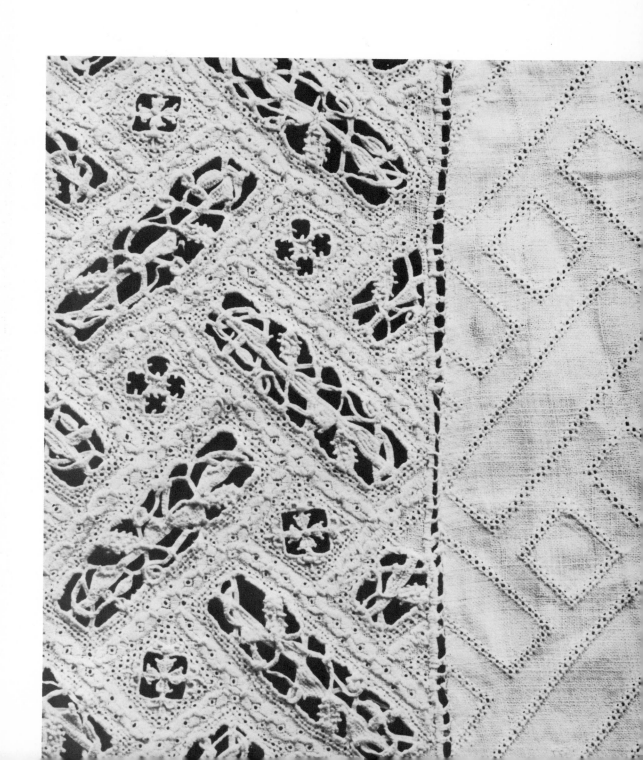

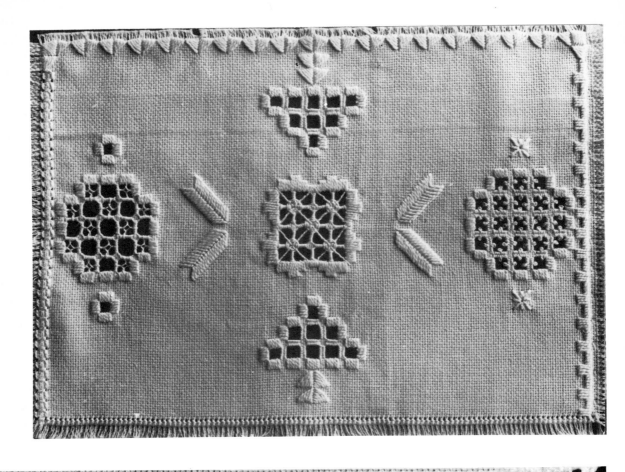

Left
Sampler of Hardanger
embroidery. This embroidery
came originally from
Norway. The holes are
created by drawn and cut
threads and the remaining
stitches are either overcast
or worked in needleweaving
with or without picots.
Satin stitch is used for the
Kloster blocks which
surround the open fillings
and for surface
embellishment. A great
variety of fillings can be
achieved by connecting the
bars or brides in different
ways and working wheels or
spider webs on the centre
crossing of the bars
Author's collection

Samplers of Hedebo
embroidery from East Prussia
worked by Frau Gombert.
The older peasant
embroidery was worked
with drawn thread and .
drawn fabric stitches, this
developed into more and
more open work with needle
lace fillings. The surface
embroidery on the later
sampler is satin stitch and
stem stitch, the filling uses
buttonhole stitch. The
embroidery came originally
from Denmark

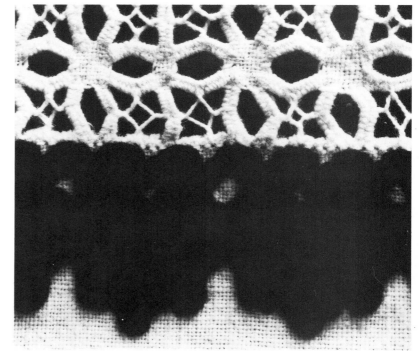

Fragment of a dress from Hungary.
Needleweaving has been worked on
threads which were left after warp and
weft threads had been drawn. The surface
embroidery is of French and bullion knots
in a heavy black thread.
Detail. The stitches which connect the
bars are worked at the same time as the
needleweaving of the bars
Embroiderers' Guild Collection

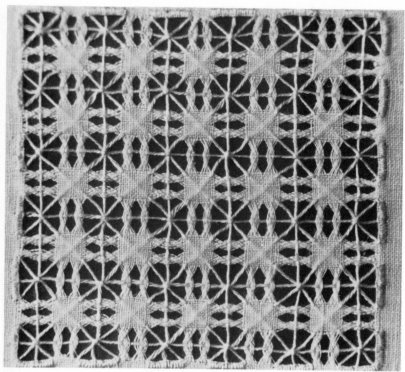

Samples of drawn thread work from
Hessen/Germany from the collection of
Frau Thekla Gombert. The larger and
more precise holes in the lower sampler
are created by overcasting the remaining
threads tightly, this is a later development
of drawn thread work

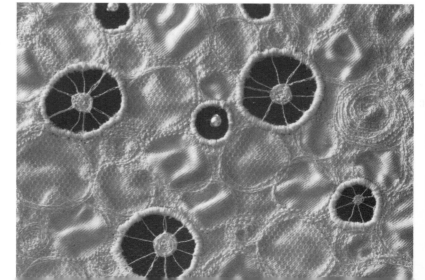

False sleeve, nineteenth century Britain. White lawn with broderie Anglaise and fine buttonhole lace fillings
Embroiderers' Guild collection

Part of a collar worked in machine cutwork. The embroidery is worked on the domestic sewing machine. Wild silk fabric is left loose under veiling which is in an embroidery frame. The circles are worked in free machining on both fabrics. The loose silk gathers under the veiling. Veiling and silk are cut away in some of the circles and the holes bound with free satin stitch. The centre of the circles is machined across the open space and in the centre in spider web, with free straight stitching. Some of the veiling is also cut away, the collar is lined with veiling on which small pearls have been sewn to show through the cut-out circles
Author's collection

Detail of embroidery on a christening gown worked around 1820 by Antonie Böse in Germany. Drawn thread work on very fine linen. The design is achieved by drawing alternate groups of warp and weft threads, working needleweaving on the remaining threads and also over the remaining squares of fabric

MBERT♥GEB♥SCHEU♥13♥2♥1833♥MANN

Family cloth worked by Frau Thekla Gombert. Family cloths were made by brides to record their family tree. The embroidery ranged from cross stitch on coarse or very fine linen to record the name and birthday of the bride, her maiden name, the date of her marriage and place to cutwork and needle point fillings of the finest workmanship

The detail shows the lace like centre worked in needleweaving on a drawn thread Russian ground edged by a row of chain stitch. Around this is worked a row of knot stitch and on the outer edge points in satin stitch. Some eyelet holes are overcast, some worked in blanket stitch. The holes in the centre of the smaller shapes are achieved by drawn thread and pulled work

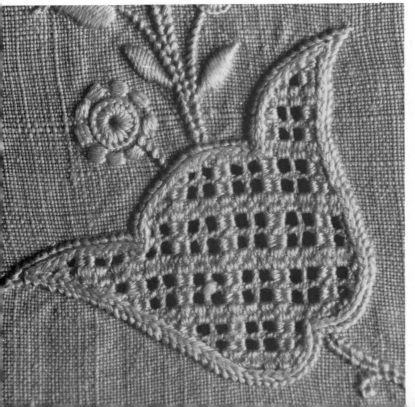

Facing page
Top The pattern in the large shape is
drawn thread work, an edging of chain
and knot stitch surrounds the shape.
Note how closely the row of knot stitch is
worked to the chain stitch. The straight
border on the left is foursided pulled or
drawn fabric stitch
Bottom Even more enlarged detail of the
cloth

Enlargements of different fillings on the
family cloth

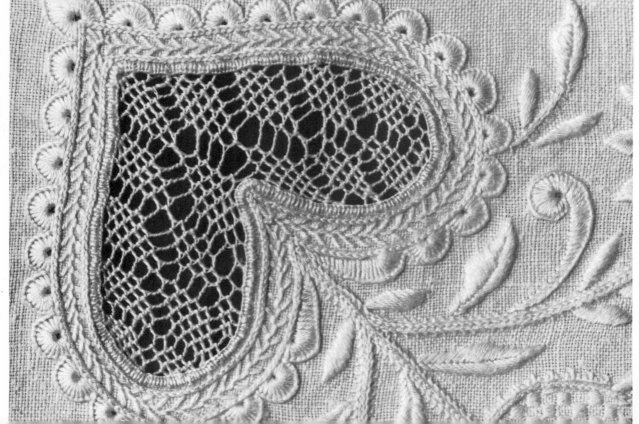

Hearts and tulips were the
traditional shapes used in the
embroidery of Schwalm/
Germany. Their origin goes
back to the middle ages. In
the older embroidery the
shapes were completely cut
out and filled with needle
point lace. The corner shape
is started by working a
buttonhole edging around
the heart shape, the edging
of the buttonhole stitch
facing the cut out area. A
row of chain stitch is then
worked close to it, feather
stitch next and chain stitch
gives the base for the
scallops which are worked
like eyelet holes. When
working the fillings the linen
is tacked to paper

A tulip motif from the same
cloth

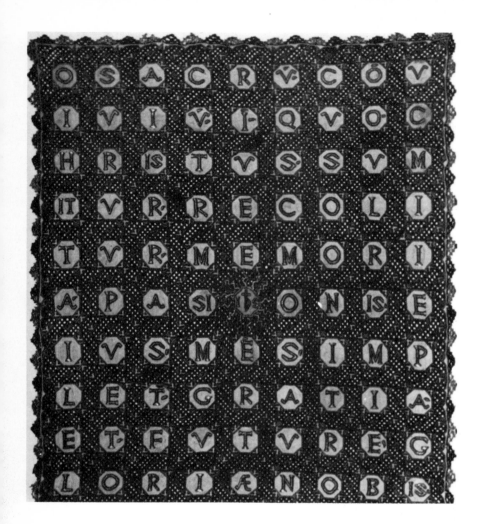

Venetian chalice veil, seventeenth century. This veil is worked in Venetian net cutwork and pulled fabric stitches to cover the background. It is worked in red silk on natural silk. The letters are padded Jap gold outlined with red silk
Textile Museum, Krefeld

Enlarged detail of the Venetian net work on the chalice veil

Drawing from a carpet from Turkestan,
first century BC. Animal motifs are
applied cloth closely quilted and outlined
by a cord formed by a twisted thread.
The carpet is quilted in spirals linked by
scrolls
Drawing by Derek Stafford

Appliqué

More and more proof for the antiquity of embroidery and specific-ally applied work has been found in the nineteenth and twentieth centuries. At Kerch on the Black Sea, in the tombs of Scythian chieftains, fragments of richly decorated textiles were found. A pall covering a woman had gold plaques applied to it and the walls were draped with embroidered hangings to which gold plaques had also been sewn. The ornaments on the plaques, as well as on the other treasures found, showed cultural influence from Greece.

By following trade routes through Manchuria to Korea, burial sites were discovered, where the graves contained fragments of ancient textiles, some of which disintegrated, when they were exposed to air. Unfortunately not much value was attached to them. The connection between the old embroideries and the life and religion of the people who made them was not appreciated. Appliqué on saddle covers, tents and carpets used by nomadic tribes who travelled in Russia from the Balkans to the Gobi desert between 200 BC and AD 220 were found in grave sites. Felt appliqué was used by all wandering cattle breeding tribes for religious and ceremonial practices, even when silk became available.

In northern Mongolia, in the Noin-Ula tombs, actual garments with gold plaques for decoration were found as well as richly embroidered wallhangings and carpets of similar Greek influence as the Kerch fragments, believed to be from the first century BC. The most interesting find was a quilted and appliquéd carpet of Scythic and Chinese influence. The quilting was in spirals linked by scrolls, the spiral being a world wide symbol, almost always found in Chinese art. The animal motifs were applied in cloth and closely quilted, outlined with a cord formed by a twisted thread. An inlaid gold plaque found at Kerch closely resembled these applied and stitched Scythian animal representations.

Fragments of Chinese Han silk (206 BC–AD 220) which had been used for patchwork on jackets and trousers, cut up and reassembled, were discovered in graves along the ancient caravan route for the silk trade from China to the West, which was opened in the second century BC and abandoned in the fourth century AD. The dating of the contents by Sir Aurel Stein was between the first and second centuries BC, contemporary with the Mongolian finds. The earliest examples of silk embroideries before the discoveries in Kerch and Mongolia were fragments of embroidered roundels illustrating Bible stories found in Coptic graves. These roundels were applied to linen garments.

During the Crusades (1095–1291) knights from Western Europe

brought back from the Middle East not only lavishly embroidered and woven fabrics, but also the fashion of wearing a surcoat decorated with appliqué which was worn over their armour to keep the sun and heat from the metal and also to identify the wearer. Heraldic appliqué, the applying of coats of arms to flags, shields and banners created a symbolic language of its own.

During the thirteenth and fourteenth centuries the superb embroidery on velvet was achieved by covering the whole surface with fine material, working the embroidery through two layers and a linen backing and then cutting away the superfluous fine fabric, again a combination of applied and cutwork. Fortunately we can still admire examples of this inspired work of the *Opus Anglicanum* period in our museums. A number of copes and vestments have survived, not only the Reformation, but also the aftermath, when precious stones and gold were removed from them and many were cut up and used for secular purposes. We must hope that methods will be found, by which these surviving pieces of evidence can be preserved for future generations without falling victim to the ravages of time.

A typical example of the method of cutting and then applying, was the embroidery of a motif with silks and metal threads on linen, which was cut out and then applied to velvet or other precious fabrics. The result was a rather clumsy piece of embroidery. From this application of motifs *raised work* developed, by padding under stitches and fabrics and finally *stumpwork* of the seventeenth century, where often whole figures were padded and applied to the background and beads were used for embellishment. Caskets and boxes were often decorated with this work. The term *appliqué* usually means the applying of one textile to another, a textile being a material fashioned by using a thread. When looking at embroidery worked in this technique, it becomes evident, that since ancient times other materials were also being used. Felt is not strictly a textile in this sense, nor is bark cloth, unless it is woven from bark fibres. These are beaten and pressed fabrics, but felt was held in high esteem and both were used for appliqué. Most elaborate appliqué and inlay work was done on skins by early man and is still being produced in northern climates, as for instance by the Eskimos and also by the shepherds in Hungary.

The appliquéd book covers of the sixteenth century, which used mainly satin and damask, also used metal threads and seed pearls. Gold spangles were used in embroidery not only by the Scythian in South Russia, but also in Babylonia, Assyria, Persia, Greece and India. The American Indians of the North West coast decorated their dance aprons which were worn at religious ceremonies, not only with applied fabrics, often felt, but with buttons, bells, shells and bands of quillwork. After contact with Europeans coloured beads were often preferred to porcupine quills. The Ainu people of Japan's main northern island Hokkaido produced a strange mixture of ancient and modern textiles. They used bark cloth with cotton trade cloth appliqué, stitched down with close rows of chain stitch and a fine cord on their wide sleeved garments, which may well have been the forerunner of the Japanese silk kimonos.

Much of the designs and techniques of the early textile fragments are also portrayed in metal work and jewellery, in ivory carving and stone sculpture of the same time in a much more complete form. This evidence supports the view that embroidery as a very old, perhaps the oldest, craft has had far reaching influence on the other crafts, whichever medium they used to picture life in the centuries gone by. The application of braids in strapwork of the fifteenth and sixteenth centuries was not confined to costume, bookcovers and ecclesiastical embroidery, but also appeared as design on wood, plaster, ivory and metal work.

Silk ribbons imported from France, around 1800, were used by the Eastern Plain and Woodland Indians of America for their very distinctive and unique ribbon embroidery. This embroidery, another example of cutting and applying, was worked by cutting designs out of a ribbon of one colour and applying not the design but the negative shape which remained, to a ribbon of another colour. Cutting a second set with the same or a mirror image of the design, but reversing the colours of the ribbons, achieved a counter-change effect. On the final piece of embroidery these sets of applied ribbons would be sewn to the background or sewn together edge to edge like patchwork. The Osage Indians of Oklahoma have perfected this craft and are still using it to decorate their dress and blankets.

Coloured cotton cloth is used in the applied work of India. Red and blue cotton cloth is applied to a white unbleached cotton background. The designs are often counterchange. The edges of the coloured cotton fabric are turned under and hemmed, showing a narrow strip of white cotton cloth. The pieces of the design are therefore not completely interlocking as in true counterchange.

In Iran, on the Caspian Sea, cut out pieces of cloth were applied to a differently coloured background, each piece outlined by cords or chain stitch. This development of the eighteenth and nineteenth centuries was known as *resht work*. It often had embroidery stitches added and resembled inlay patchwork when the pieces of applied fabric were let into the background. The designs were Persian and the embroidery was found on prayer mats and saddle cloths.

Appliqué combined with patchwork and quilting flourished in the eighteenth and nineteenth centuries in America. The English and German colonists needed protection from the cold climate and a great number of bed covers were made. From this need for warmth and the economic necessity to preserve every scrap of fabric, the art of patchwork quilts grew to a real folk art. Every girl was expected to have at least a 'baker's dozen' quilts in her dower chest. Twelve of these were for every day use and the thirteenth was the bride's quilt. This last one was not started until the girl became engaged. The others she worked in patchwork and appliqué in her girlhood. They were all stored awaiting quilting. The highest cost of the quilt was the wadding and the backing, so the quilting was not started until the time came to furnish the new home. Guests were invited to the quilting and this was as good as announcing the marriage. By exchanging fabrics and working in groups, quilt-making became a social occasion, which brought together neighbours and relatives alike. Many of the applied shapes of the American quilts were derived from simply folding paper and cutting shapes out of the folded layers. In the same way printed calico or chintzes were folded and cut. The opened out fabric shape was then sewn to the background by either blind hemming or buttonhole or blanket stitch. Sometimes flowers or animals or other designs on the chintzes were cut from the printed fabric and applied in the same way. The background could be either a single patch or block or a piece of meticulously executed patchwork. Blocks were often worked by different women in patchwork or appliqué and then in quilting sessions sewn together and quilted. Many examples of friendship quilts, where each block is signed and dated, still exist.

A similar method of making beautiful covers was used in India. Cut out shapes of cotton fabric, achieved by the same folding and cutting method, were applied to a background of a different colour, the edges turned under and the patch blindstitched or hemmed to the background. These squares of two layers of cotton, one with a cut out design applied to the other, were then joined into a patchwork cloth and a border, often in counterchange appliqué, worked around it.

Many variations of appliqué developed in the nineteenth and twentieth centuries. We have examples of carriage covers and flags from India, leather surcoats, trimmed with cloth and felt, which were ceremonial court garments in Benin, West Africa. Saddle cloth with finely worked cutwork appliqué of leather on cloth from North East Africa (Ethiopia) as well as cotton appliqué wall hangings. Felt and cotton cloth application was and is used for hats, tunics and robes all along the west coast of Africa. Some of the designs are large and crudely worked, using tinsel ribbon instead of gold and silver, others resemble the finely stitched cotton appliqué of India and also that of the Kuna Indians. Large scale appliqué was also popular in Europe around the 1880's. The designs cut out of plain fabric were applied to the background with chain stitch, and as an added decoration, herringbone stitch was worked from the edge of the chain stitch to the background.

Sabrina work used velvet, satin, silk or washable fabrics to cut out flowers, petals and leaves and widely spaced buttonhole stitch to sew them to the background.

Broderie perse was applied work in which figures, trees, flowers and animals and other objects were cut from cotton material and stitched to a plain ground or patchwork. Sprays of flowers, leaves and tendrils were cut out of fabric, pasted to another fabric and, when dry, stems, veins and stamen were embroidered. Cut flower embroidery tried to achieve a realistic effect by applying leaves, petals and flowers of the correct colour to the ground fabric.

In Hungary beautifully worked appliqué of coloured leather on sheepskin coats, which were worn with the wool inside, are survivors of the dress of shepherds of ancient times.

All these methods were used on church vestments as well as on secular articles. Some of the methods were only popular for a short time.

The land cultivating people in Europe maintained the excellence of their embroidery through the old customs of furnishing a home before marriage. In Sweden men's linen wedding shirts were magnificently embellished by the bride, so were caps worked in drawn thread in Denmark. Bodices and linen caps were worked both in linen threads and coloured wools in Norway. Household linen was marked with initials and dated, often in white work. Where traditions were carefully guarded, the craft survived in the 'peasant costume' and 'peasant embroidery' of central Europe. When the advance of machine-made goods was followed by the collapse of the apprenticeship system and the decline of home handwork, the custom of wearing national dress survived only for Sundays and special occasions.

In the second half of the nineteenth century William Morris gathered a group of artists and craftsmen around him and did more than anyone to stress the importance of individual craftwork and design in England, in an age when the machine threatened to take over. The interest in embroidery grew, Morris himself worked with textiles and designed embroideries. In London a School of Needlework was established, which concerned itself mainly with the reproduction of seventeenth century English embroidery. The influence of its teachers was felt as far afield as America. Italy opened a School of Needlework about the same time and taught girls and women who worked in the house or in the fields to use their leisure time to create beautiful embroideries which were then marketed at their fairs by societies especially set up for this purpose. Many traditional embroideries were revived by them.

Appliqué was a favourite technique in the early twentieth century in England. The interest in embroidery had been encouraged by the Needlework Development Scheme's teaching, which placed great importance on design, Art Colleges, Towns Women's Guilds, Women's Institutes, the Royal School of Needlework, which had a high reputation for meticulous technique and the Embroiderers' Guild, which not only published a magazine, but had an extensive historical collection and arranged courses and exhibitions, which it still continues to do. Great enthusiasm has been shown in church embroidery, caused by and encouraged by the refurnishing of churches which had been damaged during the second World War. Here the established symbolism of the Church has been of great help in inspiring design.

In 1962 a group of professional embroiderers joined to form the

62 Group, which has as its aim to raise the standard of embroidery, especially design and which holds exhibitions to enable its members to exhibit and sell their work. Membership is by rigid selection, to ensure a high standard of work. As a member of this group my own work, developed by incorporating the Kuna Mola technique, has been shown in some of their exhibitions.

Only future generations will be able to assess how far our achievement in embroidery has been able to convey the thoughts and ideas which moved us and which should, together with other visual artifacts, give a picture of our time.

A curious sequence of movement or pattern is evident when looking at English embroidery through the centuries. This seems to have been repeated in the twentieth century.

Religious embroidery of the early recorded pieces and of the Middle Ages led to domestic embroidery with a love for nature, flowers, gardens and animals in Elizabethan times. This was followed by elaborate embroidery with metal threads and beads and spangles culminating in embroidered boxes and caskets in the sixteenth and seventeenth centuries.

Raised work was produced next, *stumpwork* frames to mirrors, pictures with padded figures, sometimes part of the fabric tinted and painted and left to show, especially on faces. At the same time knotting made an appearance. *Berlin woolwork* spread rapidly and *canvas work* flourished. In the twentieth century in England interest in embroidery was again stimulated by church embroidery. Renewed attention was given to nature, and the use of plants and nature in general for design purposes was encouraged. A love for beads and decorated boxes was succeeded by the appearance of picture panels worked entirely in stitches or including padding and raised areas, also patchwork. From this followed three dimensional work and soft sculpture and then the introduction of painted and dyed areas on the embroidered panels. Simultaneously a vogue for knotted work (*macramé*) started and canvas work became increasingly popular. Modern stumpwork included the frequent use of mirrors decorated in this way. We seem to have gone through the same cycle of centuries ago in rather more speedy progression. Even the use of patchwork, so loved by the European emigrants in America, is enjoying a comeback.

Leaf of Consular diptych of Flavius
Anastasius, consul AD 517. Early sixth
century, Byzantine. 36·5 cm × 13 cm
(14½ in. × 5¼ in.)
Victoria and Albert Museum, London
This early carving shows lavish
decoration on the consul's gown and also
on horse trappings. These woven or
embroidered textiles must have been
made and worn well before the diptych
was carved

83

An embroidered roundel of
the saline pump in
Lüneburg, Germany. The
pump dates from 1569, the
embroidery was made in
1639. The story telling
features are embroidered in
stitchery, surrounded by a
band of applied motives.
This piece of embroidery
could have been made for
applying to brocade or
velvet to decorate a banner
or ceremonial dress
Museum in Lüneburg

Sixteenth century Italian appliqué.
Cotton and linen are applied to velvet.
The joins are covered with a couched
cord. The whole embroidery is lined with
linen
Textile Museum, Krefeld

Appliqué of red and gold couched with gold cord. Where the couched cord is missing through wear, the stitches holding the applied pieces can be seen
Textile Museum, Krefeld

A strip of appliqué on silk, the shapes are surrounded by a couched cord
Textile Museum, Krefeld

Embroidery of applied bands and strapwork surrounding shapes worked in great detail were also depicted on ivory caskets and silver workings. Hispano-Arabic (Cordoba) early eleventh century. The silver which is engraved was probably added in the seventeenth or eighteenth century
Victoria and Albert Museum, London

Aino Kimono. The Aino are a race which antedates the Japanese people with a high artistic culture. Only few specimens of their culture have survived. The garment is made from attush, a cloth woven from the inner bark of elm trees, with cotton appliqué and elaborate stitchery in chain stitch

Canadian blanket, woollen cloth or felt
with button appliqué
Drawing by Derek Stafford

Facing page
Ribbon appliqué. The drawing shows the
counterchange effect achieved by
applying the shapes cut out of one ribbon
onto another and also using the
remaining ribbon for applying to yet
another one. The embroidery is finished
by sewing all the ribbons together. The
pattern was taken from an Osage Indian
blanket
Ribbon appliqué on felt. Probably Osage
Indian, Oklahoma
Textile Museum, Krefeld

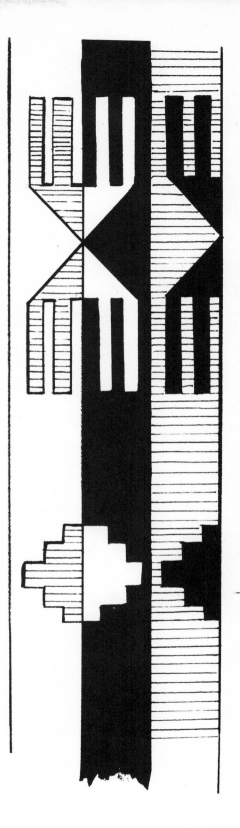

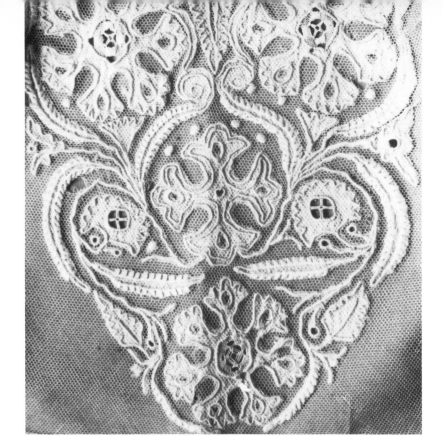

European bonnet. Cotton is applied
behind a net ground, secured with
whipping and flat stitches, excess cotton
is cut away at the back. To give a more
open and lacelike effect both cotton and
net are removed from small areas. Some
lace fillings in these areas are worked
mainly in buttonhole stitch. The bonnet
has been lined to support the frail
embroidery
Embroiderers' Guild collection

The ivory Hispano-Arabic casket from
Cordoba AD 975 shows the lacelike
structure with similar symbols

The hemmed appliqué on this mat from
Hungary is traditional to the countries of
eastern Europe where cut paper designs
are also traditional and obviously
influence the designs. The design is
traced onto a piece of lawn and *backed*
with a piece of net. The design is then
cut, turned with the needle and hemmed
all in one operation, but working only a
small piece of the design at a time. This is
the same working method the Kuna
Indians use and which is described in
detail
Embroiderers' Guild collection

91

Boy's hood, probably eastern Bihar worked in the early nineteenth century. White cotton appliqué on black cotton. The frill around the crown is red, the cap is bound with red and yellow piping. The white cotton appliqué is continuous and must have been cut from one piece of fabric and applied with almost invisible hemstitches

Victoria and Albert Museum, London

Indian cushion from Rajastan worked in white cotton appliqué on red cotton. The patterns were probably achieved by folding cotton and cutting the design through several layers

By courtesy of Joss Graham

93

Canopy for a Hackery carriage. Bombay c1867. The appliqué is yellow, red and white on navy blue. The bottom layer is white. The appliqué consists of two layers in any one place. On the border the first layer is exposed by cutting back to it from the top layer, turning under a seam allowance and applying the fabric with small hemstitches. Coloured patches are often added to the centre of shapes, and to the border bands, including shisha glass
Victoria and Albert Museum, London

Quilted hanging or bed cover from Sindh, Pakistan, from the mouth of the river Indus. The patterned squares are made by folding squares of cotton fabric and cutting shapes from the folded edges. The squares are then unfolded and applied to the background fabric. Coloured circles are applied next. The patterned bands are treated in the same way. Some are worked in patchwork. The running stitches hold together and quilt the embroidered top layer, a lining and an inner layer of wool or fabric
Collection of Mrs Ronnie Winship, USA

96

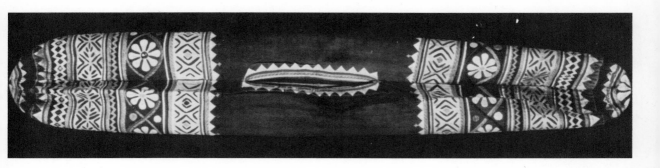

The quilt and one square in detail. The background fabric is black with squares of yellow, red, white and green cotton

Bridegroom's bag from Rajastan/India in two layer cutwork with appliqué in red, yellow and blue handwoven cotton. Detail
By courtesy of Joss Graham

Facing Page
Baltimore bride's quilt. This American
quilt shows the combination of
patchwork, appliqué and quilting. On
some of the squares the applied fabric
was folded and cut to give the
symmetrical shapes. It was then applied.
Variations of fret, cross and spiral are
symbols used for the designs. The
quilting is worked in diagonal rows of
running stitch

Detail. Two different forms of appliqué
are worked on the corner of this square.
The border scroll is applied with invisible
hemstitching. Some of the shapes of the
scroll have been cut back to a differently
coloured patch. Around the individual
squares of the quilt a border of
patchwork has been worked. One of the
three leaves inside the patchwork corner
is applied by overcasting the edge
The American Museum in Britain, Bath

98
I-15
119.

100

Benin brass plaque. Playing gongs from West Africa. This brass plaque shows ceremonial garments with appliqué. These plaques exist from the sixteenth century
British Museum, London

Ceremonial court garment. Rawhide bands are covered with an applied zigzag line of rolled red woollen cloth on natural cotton with bells attached, faced with red woollen cloth. The same rolled felt cloth is applied on the main part of the garment on natural cotton fabric. The centre part of this has triangles sewn to the front with long stitches in cotton thread. Around the zigzag bands are two rolls of cloth, one red, one natural applied with hemstitching. A red cloth border completes the garment
British Museum, London

Yoruba priest's kilt. Red leather appliqué on green leather couched with maroon wool. The interlacing has rows of machining. The patterns and symbols on these ceremonial garments have been handed on from craftsman to craftsman. Although they convey myth and magic their exact meaning cannot be given. Interlacing conveys infinity, lizards fertility and hearts the soul, courage or strength of a man
Lagos Museum, Nigeria

Priest's kilt with couched lace and string with sequins. Yellow and green leather is applied to black woollen fabric, the heart motifs convey strength and the lizards stand for fertility. Many items which came from the white man were incorporated, because they were believed to give them the power of the white man
Lagos Museum

Facing page
Saddle cloth Gara Esun. Green leather is
cut back to the red layer below, the
stitches applying the leather are covered
by a couched yellow cord. Herringbone
stitching and pattern darning is worked
in maroon wool
Lagos Museum

Tribal gathering in north eastern Nigeria
to celebrate the coronation of a new Emir.
The garments of the men on foot are
appliquéd, also the sleeves of the men on
horses. Some of the horse trappings go
back to the thirteenth century. The
saddle cloths are also worked in leather
appliqué
Jeanette Durrant

Facing page
A Dahomey (Benin) funeral hanging. This hanging would be hung as a memorial in a mud shrine. The appliqué of 'Sacrifice of a cow' is worked on fine cotton. The applied cotton features have turned under and finely stitched hems. Probably made in 1960. Other objects in the hanging symbolise events in the man's life. The cow is red cotton on black cloth, the light colour is yellow
Lagos Museum

Funeral shrine hanging. Ibibio Nwomo Monuments. From the eastern regions. These were hung in outside shrines in dense tropical bush. They would be left there to rot and would not last longer than about six months under those conditions. The appliqué cut-outs are tacked to the background. Mirror, umbrellas, guns and hats all symbolise man's status. The fabrics used were probably exported from Holland for African markets
All Lagos photographs by Jeanette Durrant, Lagos Museum

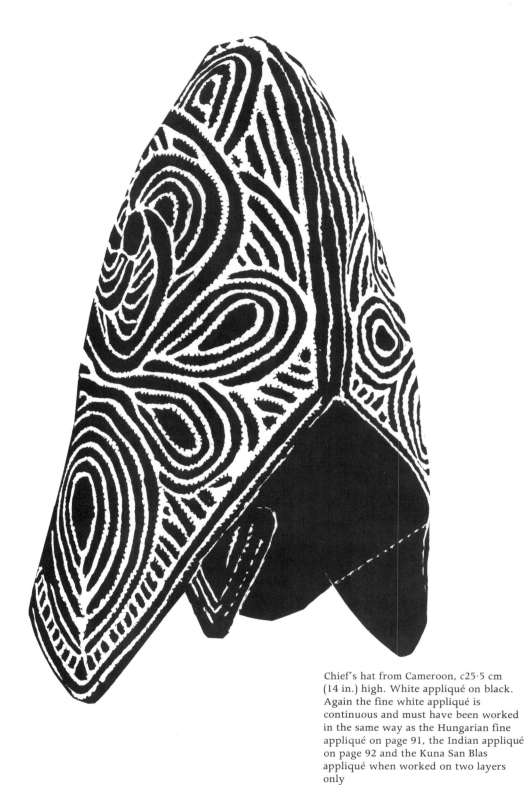

Chief's hat from Cameroon, c25·5 cm
(14 in.) high. White appliqué on black.
Again the fine white appliqué is
continuous and must have been worked
in the same way as the Hungarian fine
appliqué on page 91, the Indian appliqué
on page 92 and the Kuna San Blas
appliqué when worked on two layers
only

Ceremonial fan, Nigeria. Dyed goat-skin.
Applied cloth and mirrors

Facing page
Nineteenth century English appliqué.
Designed and worked by N H Baillie
Scott in 1896
Victoria and Albert Museum, London

A cushion cover, Scottish. Designed and
worked by Jessie R Newberry. Applied
work on linen with needleweaving and
satin stitch in coloured silks
Victoria and Albert Museum, London

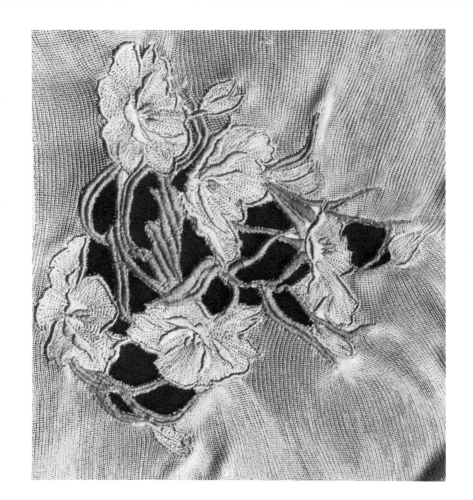

A combination of appliqué and cutwork by Karen Nicol. Plain and pleated knitted fabric had silk applied by free machining. The decorative stitching is satin stitch and free straight stitch. The silk and knitted fabric is cut away in certain areas. Approx size of motif 15·2 cm (6 in.)

Twentieth century appliqué by Heather Clarke. 'In the Pink' 44·5 cm × 54·6 cm (17½ in. × 21½ in.). Machine and hand appliqué. Patterned fabrics and velvet are used, some with padding and some hand stitchery

'Belle Vue', 21·5 cm (8½ in.) square by
Heather Clarke is a combination of
cutwork and appliqué. The appliqué is
padded and has surface stitches added

Machine applied fabric shapes are used
on the panel by Richard Box. 'Danae'
approx 61 cm × 45·7 cm (24 in. × 18 in.).
The figure is silver kid padded and
applied

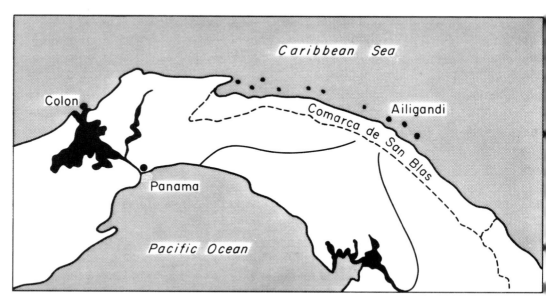

Central Panama
Kuna Indians live in the Comarca de San Blas
and on the coastal islands

The Kuna Indians
and their Mola embroidery

I found the 'embroidery' or better 'stitchery' of the Kuna Indian molas an ideal way of linking cutwork and appliqué and an interesting example of the development of craft and design in an environment, which was only superficially influenced by Western contact. Perhaps I was also moved by the inconsistency with which some of the early descriptions of their textiles were treated. For instance: Professor Henry Wassén quotes Erland Nordenskiöld's description (1930) of picture-writing on balsa wood boards which he compares with picture-writing on paper collected among the San Blas Kuna and points out the close similarities. He then writes: 'I therefore think that we are quite entitled to consider even these paintings on balsa wood planks as real picture-writing and not pure design as for instance the ornaments on the women's molas or blouses.' (*Etnologiska Studier* 16 Henry Wassén.) The same view was held by Ruben Perez Kantule, a Kuna Indian, who had been invited by Nordenskiöld and who went to Gothenburg in Sweden to record as much as he could remember of the past and present history of his people. He reported that, although the decoration on the molas had no magic and did not frighten the spirits, in some areas the women turned their molas inside out when in the presence of a person who had been bitten by a snake, because the figures with which they were ornamented might otherwise do harm to the sick man and prevent him from recovering! He did admit the importance of being able to make beautiful objects by suggesting that medicine made from the exquisitely designed leaves of the Sappi Karta tree should be used. One artist, who bathed his eyes with this, was able to draw better, make all kinds of beautiful baskets and cut unusually beautiful molas.

After examining a collection of rare molas in the British Museum and in the Ethnographic Museum in Gothenburg in Sweden, I felt compelled to find out and record all available information about this art and its origin. After several years of study, my husband and I visited the beautiful San Blas islands on the Caribbean coast of Panama.

We stayed on the island of Ailigandi, one of the more easterly islands, where we met and were welcomed by the Indians. In the tropical setting of palm trees, the deep green foliage of the vegetation, the natural colour of the palm thatched huts which are built of golden bamboo cane, the clean white coral beaches and the clear blue to dark green sea, the graceful women in their many coloured molas provided the splash of colour which completed an enchanting picture. Taken out of this background into our environment, although still beautiful, they seem to clash with the multitude of colours and shapes that assail our eyes.

A mola is made up of two rectangular panels, front and back. These are made to fit the size of the girl or woman. They are joined by a seam on each side and then attached to a yoke of plain or patterned cotton, but now sometimes made of man-made fibre. The finished garment has a bound neck opening, which can be adjusted by a drawstring to fit the wearer and a short plain or gathered set-in sleeve. The shoulder has always some appliqué in the form of an epaulette and the lower edge has a narrow frill attached to it, which helps to keep it inside the skirt. This blouse is tucked into a wrap around skirt which is calf to ankle length and made from printed patterned cotton trade cloth. A printed bright yellow and red headscarf is always worn by married women, either covering the head or carried folded up on the shoulder. The outfit is completed by patterned beaded arm and leg bands and gold and silver jewellery. This costume is their every day attire, although Western dress is also worn, often in combination with the mola. *Mola* is a Kuna Indian word for cloth. It is often used to describe either the complete blouse, or the two rectangular embroidered panels, or just one of these panels, which have now become highly prized collectors items.

From the time we first knew about the Indians in the sixteenth century, their rediscovery in the nineteenth century and their life now, we can trace many factors which have led to changes in their dress and its embellishment. Many links in this chain of events are still missing and some of the early reports are suspect because of the prejudice of the writer and the image he wanted to present to his people at home. The evidence which is available clearly shows an adaptation to the environment and the influence of outside contact.

The Indians first met white people in the sixteenth century, when the Spaniards, who had sailed to the West Indies and from there to Panama were welcomed by the Indians and led to the Pacific coast of Panama. These meetings were disastrous for the local inhabitants who were exploited and enslaved in the Spanish search for Eldorado. The chieftains and culture which had existed before the Spaniards came, were destroyed. The few Indians who had escaped the massacre and slavery and had fled into the mountains, reverted to a simpler pattern of existence, but here some of the native culture survived. These tribes had a reputation of being savage and dangerous and were therefore not molested by the Spaniards, negros, nor future Scottish, French and English invaders. These were the tribes who found and looked after an English pirate surgeon Lionell Wafer. He had sustained an accidental gun powder wound to his knee and had been left behind by his expedition on their return journey from the Pacific coast of Panama to the Caribbean. In the four months he spent with the Indians in the mountains, they looked after him, cured his wound and later guided him and four of his companions across the cordillera back to the Caribbean.

No Indians lived on the islands on the Caribbean coast at that time. He noted and recorded not only his great surprise at their superior medical knowledge but also everything around him. He learned their language and took part in their customs, especially bodypainting and wrote the first reliable report in 1681, published in 1699, nine years after he had returned to England. He not only described the fine long black and white gowns with fringes that were worn by the chieftains and their attendants on special occasions, but also in detail the spinning, weaving and dyeing of cotton for cloth and hammocks. We learn from him how the Kunas obtained their dyes from wood and vegetable matter and also from earth, which they used for their bright and elaborate tattooing and body painting. This was done in their favourite colours of blue-black, red and yellow. Apart from these ceremonial garments the Indians wore a nose decoration in the shape of a large golden disk, which Wafer also adopted and golden and beaded ornaments around neck, arms and legs. Men wore a cone shaped penis cover or a breech clout and women a kneelength skirt. Bishop Dr Lucas Fernandes y Piedrahita, who lived about the same time as Wafer, noted in his Historia General de la Conquista del Nuevo Mundo y Reino Granada, that although the Darien men went naked, the women were always modestly clothed in cotton garments curiously embroidered. We shall, of course, never know what he understood by embroidery. The ceremonial garments and gold, silver, animal teeth and feather adornments described by Wafer show the significance of distinguishing rank, whereas the tattooing and body painting seemed to him to be only decoration. He described in detail the nature of the painting men had applied to them by their women folk before they went to war. The brush they used for this purpose was made by chewing a stick until it resembled a brush. 'Birds, Beasts, Men, Trees or the like up and down in every part of the body, more especially on the face. The figures are not extraordinary like what they represent, and are of differing Dimensions as their fancies lead them.' He did not know, that the Kuna religion endows every human, animal and plant with a purba or soul, so that animals and plants could be images of spirits. It was common to portray these spirits and their abodes in tattooing and bodypainting.

In an uprising, which started in 1726, of the whole of the Darien population against Spanish and French colonists, some of whom had mixed with the Indians, all the French were massacred in 1757. When, in 1790, Spain withdrew all garrisons and abandoned all forts in Darien, the Kunas had once more reasserted their immunity. We know from Dampier's Voyage Round the World that European buccaneers, privateers and companies in the late seventeenth and early eighteenth centuries traded extensively with the Indians and that they brought among presents scissors, beads, knives and cloth. Wafer had already noticed how pleased the women were by gifts of clothing, especially of 'gaudy' colour.

Between these first reports and the scientific expeditions which went to Panama in the twentieth century lies a big void. Before a scientific ethnographic expedition led by Erland Nordenskiöld went to Panama in the 1930s a British explorer Mitchel Hedges with Lady Richmond Brown sailed to Panama from England. They were received by the Kuna Indians on the San Blas islands in 1922. They were treated with great friendliness and invited to visit the 'savage braves' in the mountains. They made the arduous trek into the jungle and swampy interior to the upper reaches of the Chucunaque river where they met the Indians. According to the book by Lady Richmond Brown *Unknown Tribes Uncharted Seas* which was published in 1924, the mountain Indians had never seen a white man or woman in living memory. They were able to help the Indians cure some of the ailments which abounded by administering some of the drugs they had come equipped with and were showered with gifts as a reward. They brought back a whole collection of artifacts which were then distributed among several museums in England and the United States. In her book she gives a travelogue type of report of their adventures with excellent photographs of the islands, its people and their molas. This book, which is long out of print, I found to my great surprise and delight accidentally in my father-in-law's stowed away collection of books!

Lady Richmond Brown is in fact the first person I know, who was interested enough in the embroidery to describe accurately and photograph the blouses. She even made an effort to trace the meaning and origin of the designs after she had returned to England. There is a lengthy dissertation on the relationship of designs on molas with Maya calendrical signs by Ludovic MacLellan Mann, who was president of the Glasgow Archaeological Society from 1931–1933, quoted in her book. She refers to the dress of the Kantules (Medicine men and chanters) 'They were dressed to the knees in long garments entirely covered with cabalistic characters and what looked like the signs of the zodiac, all in some way or other worked into, or let into, the cloth in a form of patchwork. I can think of no other way to describe it. It must be seen to be understood.'

The dates of the collection in the British Museum are, of course, the dates on which these items were received. There are about 170 garments of varied design, some very simple, others more complicated, with no clue when they were made. Neither were any of the comments made about the embroidery by Lady Richmond Brown recorded. I found this very puzzling, as her findings agree exactly with later discoveries and observations by the Swedes.

Could it be that a divorced woman, who was an amateur and went on an expedition with a man, was not considered trustworthy in Victorian minded England in 1922?

She writes in her book that the Kuna women stored the finished garments in calabashes and so preserved them from the climate in the tropical rainforests, but this gives no clue as to when they were actually made. The oldest mola I know about is in the Smithsonian Institution in Washington. This was collected by Eleanor Bell. She

Abstract mola depicting devils *Ethnographic Museum, Gothenburg* ▶

writes in the Smithsonian Institution Annual Report of 1909 that the fabric used was 'Cotton Cloth of English Manufacture'. I have not been able to get any positive evidence that the material used on the British Museum molas was also made in England. It would be very interesting if it had, as this cloth would have to have been traded by the island Indians from Europe or the United States and then carried to the mountain tribes.

E Y Bell thought that the garments were identical with the ones Wafer had described. As far as I could find, Wafer did not describe embroidery in detail, so the assumption that they were made as far back as the seventeenth century seems inadequately supported. It is quite possible that close identification was very difficult before 1900 because the Indians would not allow any white person to stay on the islands or in the mountains, certainly not overnight, nor let any man get near their women folk.

David Stout wrote in 1947 that there is no mention of Indians on the islands until well into the nineteenth century and that before 1741 no colonisation of the islands had taken place. Missionaries arrived on the islands around 1900.

When Erland Nordenskiöld and his expedition went to Panama to research into Kuna mythology, the Indians were well established on some fifty of the 360 or so islands near the mouths of the rivers. These coral islands had no fresh water nor firewood. This had to be fetched from the mainland daily. The tribal communities led by *caciques* (chieftains) farmed on the mainland and traded with passing ships from many countries, using their coconut crop as currency. Farming, hunting and fishing made them completely self sufficient. Life on the climatically healthier islands probably started as an escape from the malaria ridden swamps and jungles of the mainland. The Indians had a highly developed sense of independence, their own language, religion and style of life. They had deliberately kept out foreigners and only accepted from the little contact they had had, what fitted into their already held beliefs. In 1925 they had regained their right for self-government from Panama.

The only written language was picture writing on balsa wood and later on paper with coloured pencils which they had traded. This writing was at first thought to be pure design or just an aid to memory for the chanters or Kantules but after extensive research with the help of educated Indians, the Swedish ethnographers and linguists found that they could translate the symbols. They were songs which were chanted at healing and puberty ceremonies. Some of the symbols portrayed devils and evil spirits. When these were tattooed or painted on the body the wearer became protected. The black line which is still painted on the nose of girls is such a design. It was originally a stylised lizard which saved souls from being taken by evil spirits or devils. Small children and babies are often painted black all over to make them invisible to these spirits. The Kunas believed that when a person became ill, the soul or purba

◀ Modern geometric design mola

was abducted by the evil spirits. Through the incantations the good spirits were induced to leave their homes and enter the wooden figures or nuchus which the medicine man had carved for this purpose and so help him to bring back the ravished soul and cure the sick. The figures were able to go down as far as the fifth layer of the nether world to help resist the evil spirits. After the ceremony the nuchus, having served their purpose, were burnt or destroyed. Although Professor Wassén of the Ethnographic Museum in Gothenburg regards the designs of the balsa wood picture writing as true picture writing and rejects the idea that the designs on the molas are more than pure design, many of the symbols on the blouses bear a striking resemblance to the picture writing.

Explanations of the origin of these designs are many and they vary from one source to another. The Indians themselves cannot explain the old symbols, many of which they still use. For enough money they will tell the inquirer any story he would like to hear. Contact with Europeans centuries ago may have planted the first seed for their writing and mola making. It is generally thought, that the mola making coincided with the move to the islands. Here the climate was fresher and the supplies of cotton cloth from trading ships much easier to obtain. Did the Indians transfer the religious symbols of their body painting to the embroidery?

The soul of a dead person on its way to heaven has to journey through the fourth layer of the eight layers of the underworld. This is where the chiefs of the evil spirits reside. Could it be, that this is represented in the mola embroidery, which often uses four layers of cotton with symbols of devils cut back to the bottom layer? Is it so far fetched, when we consider how our ancestors used embroidery to express their religious beliefs? Probably these thoughts are pure conjecture and the answer will remain a mystery.

David Stout quotes from one source in 1947: 'Kuna women in 1868 were wearing "short sleeved chemises extending to the knees". Sixty years ago (1887) this mola was of plain, usually dark blue material with a simple band of red cloth around the bottom. It reached to the knees and was worn with a knee-length underskirt painted with geometric designs. Forty to fifty years ago, women began to use brighter coloured cloth when it became accessible through the traders and to decorate the blouse along the hem with a simple appliqué of contrasting colours. The appliqué technique itself appears to have been an indigenous development. Within a few years the appliqué covered the lower half of the mola. About forty years ago (1907) the trading boats presented figured blue trade cloth which soon became to be used as a wrap-around skirt, as a result of which the mola became shorter, the appliqué portion moved upwards so that today only a short bodice is of plain cloth and the practice of painting the underskirt was discontinued.' (Stout 1947:67.) Nordenskiöld seemed to think that the appliqué technique was 'an imitation of something else one had seen among white people' and 'that about 50 years ago (1878) the cloth was painted and before that they naturally had handwoven cloth.'

The Kuna Indian missionary Peter Miller, who was 69 when I met him in 1975, could remember his grandmother sewing molas. That would be somewhere around 1880 and that is as near as I have come to the starting date of mola making.

I find it fascinating that such a unique and elaborate embroidery has been developed by a people who have until very recently not caught up with the sophistication of Western life.

To summarize: We know that apart from the protective function of the Kuna costume its colour and decoration denoted rank during ceremonies and festivals. The decoration was heraldic and consisted of the painting of stylised animal, human and plant forms on body and cloth. Men dressed according to the position they held in the tribe. Women wore the colourful molas according to the demands of traditional occasions.

Although life is changing fast on these tranquil and beautiful islands, many of the old customs are still adhered to. The Kuna women still wear a thick gold nose ring and large, flat disk shaped gilded earrings. This attractive custom is disappearing rapidly. Since the Spaniards misused the gold they found in Panama the Kuna do not make their own jewellery, it has to be bought and is usually made by Chinese craftsmen. Molas are sewn all the time and everywhere by women and sometimes men. For special occasions, such as independence festivities or puberty celebrations, the women will design and work in secret on molas which are displayed during the festivities and the dancing on the actual day. These different molas, all inspired by the same conception are much sought after by collectors. The quality of design is still high, even when the sewing machine is used to sew up the side seams and rickrack braid incorporated in the mola panel. In quite a number of huts a Singer sewing machine is part of the furniture. To attempt the embroidery on the machine would need as much practice and skill as handstitching, but I have seen a few attempts. No great importance is attached to the yoke or the frill of the blouse. Most unsuitable materials and colours are being used for these. Contrary to their marvellous sense of colour on the panels, the frills and yokes do not seem to harmonise with the rest of the garment, at least to my Western orientated eye. They will often re-use a panel by attaching it to a new yoke.

All the collections I have seen consist of a variety of different types. The older molas collected in the mountains of Colombia are often simple geometric designs, sometimes only worked as borders at the hem of the blouse.

I do not think that we can find proof of the development of the mola from a very simple form to the highly ornate one in slow, clearly defined stages. It seems likely that important symbols were first used in repetition across a piece of fabric which could be made to fit any size woman, often in two layers only. A later stage of fitting the design into a pre-determined size developed into an

123

organised panel. The latest form of mola designing is story telling.

There could also be purely practical reasons for some features of the designs. The stitching together of up to four or five layers of cloth produces a very rigid textile, which would be quite uncomfortable when performing manual tasks. The obvious thing to do is to make it more flexible by cutting and sewing vertical slashes through to the layer nearest the body. The Kuna woman often cuts and sews the large shapes of her design to the bottom layer, works the following layers by keeping the base layer exposed right through the top layer and so achieves quite a considerable measure of elasticity and stretch. The cut-out shapes of the first panel are used on the second panel, thus effecting great economy in the use of fabric and creating the front and back of the garment which are similar but not alike. An old Indian motto is that only God is perfect and a small imperfection is incorporated in each piece of work.

The well constructed mola will not have any protruding areas as these would wear first and rub off during laundering. They are therefore applied to any but the top layer. Large empty spaces in the work are undesirable. They would leave the cloth loose and so again make it wear out more quickly. The embroidery stitches the Indians used on the old molas did nothing more than hold the layers together where it was too difficult to cut further. These have now developed into quite elaborate embellishment.

Fabrics are expensive and treasured and the Kuna woman is very thrifty. Every scrap of fabric is saved and stored in the baskets her menfolk weave. She often uses the scraps on the second or third layer of her work. Between two layers the patches do not become uncomfortable in wear nor do they get torn away or frayed when washed. The mola is only lined if the fabric used is too flimsy to make a strong blouse. The design is always stitched through the lining. Tourist demand has made many of the practical considerations unnecessary and when working for the tourist trade much more appliqué is used on the top layer. This is of course quicker than working the design through the layers. Unfortunately copying of whole molas has started, where before only a main part of a design would be handed on. The tourist demand has led to the making of single panels and the production of much cruder designs which are also quicker to work. On their own dress molas women might spend up to two years, stitching only when they feel inspired to work. By the display of molas on the islands and in Panama City and the determined effort of the women to sell their work to the tourists they can earn enough money to buy more cloth for more mola making. They are very shrewd traders and bargain for the highest price they can get and sometimes when a price has been apparently agreed on, they change their mind and refuse to sell. By forcefully resisting the alien influence and moving away from the invaders, the Kuna Indians have been able to rebuild a stable, self-sufficient society which can hold its own and has, up to now, been respected by its neighbours. Hopefully they will come to terms with all the technical innovations that Western society is bound to introduce. There are still islands where the aeroplane and the missionary doctor are not allowed to go. Schools, both Panamanian and Mission have been established on a number of islands. Mola making is not only taught in a family setting but by Kuna teachers in the schools.

In the near future they will have to face and come to terms with technical development that the newly opened dam on the Bayano river will bring, the possibility of road building to the Caribbean coast and worst of all the rather more remote chance that a new Panama Canal will be built, cutting through their territorial region. All these developments are in abeyance at present because of the impenetrable jungle between their land, the islands and the Pacific. Even the last stretch of the Pan American Highway in this area has not been built because of these difficulties. At the moment the only communication is by small trading boats in the Caribbean and a limited service by aeroplanes carrying six to seven passengers to short primitive landing strips on the coast and from there by dug-out canoe or cayuca to the islands.

With their strong feeling of unity they may be able to withstand the onslaught of Western commercial greed and exploitation.

Facing page
Kuna woman wearing her mola blouse with pelican design tucked into her printed wrap-around cotton skirt. The yoke of the mola is covered by necklaces made from American silver coins, her bracelets and anklets are small trade beads threaded in traditional pattern. Her married status is shown by the headscarf she wears over her short hair. Large goldplated earrings and a golden nose ring complement her straight black hair and her light brown skin

A 'dog mola' from Achutupo, San Blas. This mola is worked in two layers only. The zigzag or saw tooth lines attaching the panels to the yoke are stitched but manufactured rick-rack braid is used on the sleeves and the body of the yoke. Running stitch in different colours holds the two layers together on the larger uncut areas of the top layer. The frill which finished the lower edge has been removed

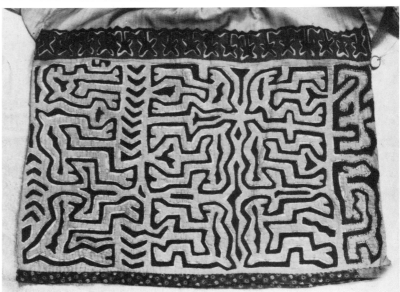

The front and back of a mola collected by Lady Richmond Brown in 1922. It is worked in three layers. The lower edge is bound with blue and white printed fabric. Patterned printed materials are often used in the old molas, either for a complete layer or for patches between the layers

British Museum, London

Drawing of a mola described by Eleanor
Yorke Bell in 1909. The figure supposedly
human, is much more likely to be a
tutelary spirit, drawn and embroidered to
protect the wearer. Figures like the one
on the mola are a common feature of
picture writing

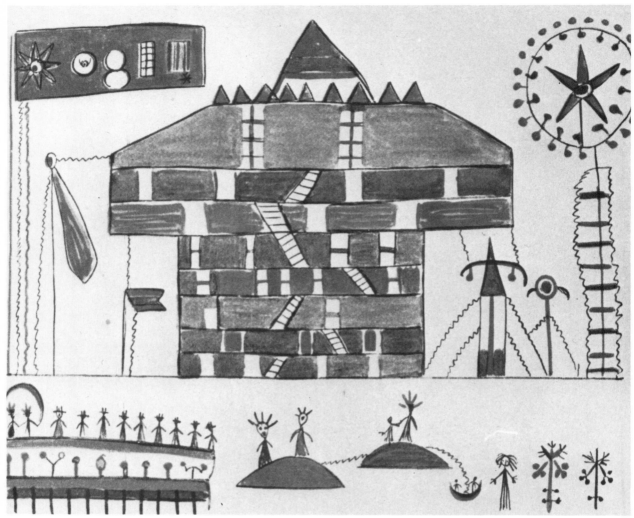

Picture writing. The soul of a deceased Indian goes on a long journey before it reaches heaven, guided by the tutelary spirits who help it overcome the obstacles. He reaches a point of high elevation from which the earth looks no larger than a quarter of a coconut and in heaven he sees great palaces where golden eagles abound.
Ethnographic Museum, Gothenburg

The all important zigzag line which stands for the umbilical cord, so important in the story of creation of the Kuna mythology and which is also a symbol of fertility in other cultures

Molas which use picture writing symbols.
The house or palace of heaven.
Eagles standing on lizards
British Museum, London

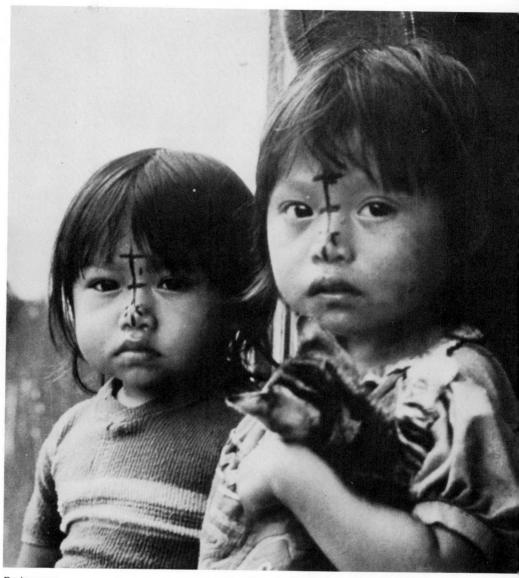

Facing page
Top 'Nia 'Djavul' or devil mola
Ethnographic Museum, Gothenburg
Bottom The lobster demon is a demon
who obstructs childbirth. He holds on to
the child during a breach delivery
British Museum, London
All evil spirits can be defeated if they are
portrayed. This was formerly done by
bodypainting

Two Kuna Indian girls from Ailigandi.
The black line on their noses is a stylised
lizard and is drawn on girls' noses to
protect them from evil spirits

133

134

Facing page
Nuchus. These are wooden carved figures into which the good spirits are induced to enter by the incantations of the medicine man. They help him to bring back the soul of the sick. They were often carved dressed in old European dress
Ethnographic Museum, Gothenburg

A modern nuchu for tourists. Like the ceremonial ones it is carved from balsa wood and painted

135

Another piece of picture writing from: The journey through the next world by Néle. It describes the journey of the soul after death. The tutelary spirits of the bottom row (which is always the row where the reading starts) help the soul to cross a lake. They throw a thread across which changes into a bridge. Cotton cords as well as ladders are placed in the graves to be carried by the dead soul on its travels

A mola depicting a fight with a fish.
This is an example of the latest stage of
mola making – story telling
By courtesy of Mrs Ann Bryant, USA

Facing page
A symbol connected with childbirth is
the turtle. Moromunéki is the great turtle
demon who obstructs delivery so that the
woman can only move her hands. Jaw
bones of the great turtle are given as
medicine. This mola shows the fine
quality of the embroidery and the rather
crude sewing of the garment
British Museum, London

Another much cruder example of the
same symbol collected at the same time.
It is worked in five layers
British Museum, London

The inside of the mola. The tracery of the
stitching is almost as beautiful as the
outside of the embroidery

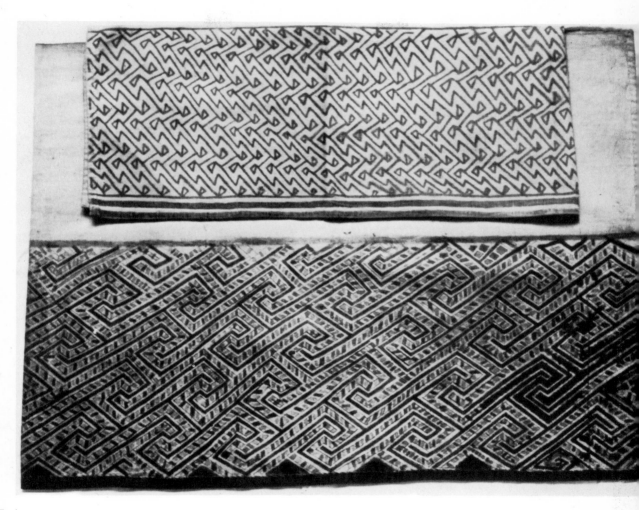

Facing page
The turtle symbol is still used today. This beautifully worked mola from Karti–San Blas, the most westerly group of islands, shows the more widespread use of stitchery on modern molas

Hand printed cotton skirts from San Blas. This hand printing is thought to have preceded mola making and replaced body painting
Ethnographic Museum, Gothenburg

Figure with body painting and patterned
textile skirt from Panama
British Museum, London
Kuna Indian woman wearing her mola
and all her traditional ornaments

Facing page and colour overleaf
Mola from the Rio Caiman on the Gulf of
Uraba, Colombia. A border at the bottom
of the skirt is thought to have led to a
wider and wider area of embroidery until
the complete skirt part of the garment
had been covered. The very simple cross
and fret pattern could be worked in the
first method of Kuna appliqué described,
by cutting back from the top layer to the
second layer and from the second to the
first
Ethnographic Museum, Gothenburg

Mola using cross symbols and saw-tooth edging from Colombia. The appliqué is only a border at the bottom of the garment and worked in simple shapes with wide margins. The Kuna Indians of these eastern and mountain regions have not developed their mola technique as much as the western regions. Another explanation for the more simple designs could be, that these molas were made a long time ago.
Ethnological Museum, Gothenburg

Cotton with small print was widely used, frequently for the botton layer
British Museum, London

144

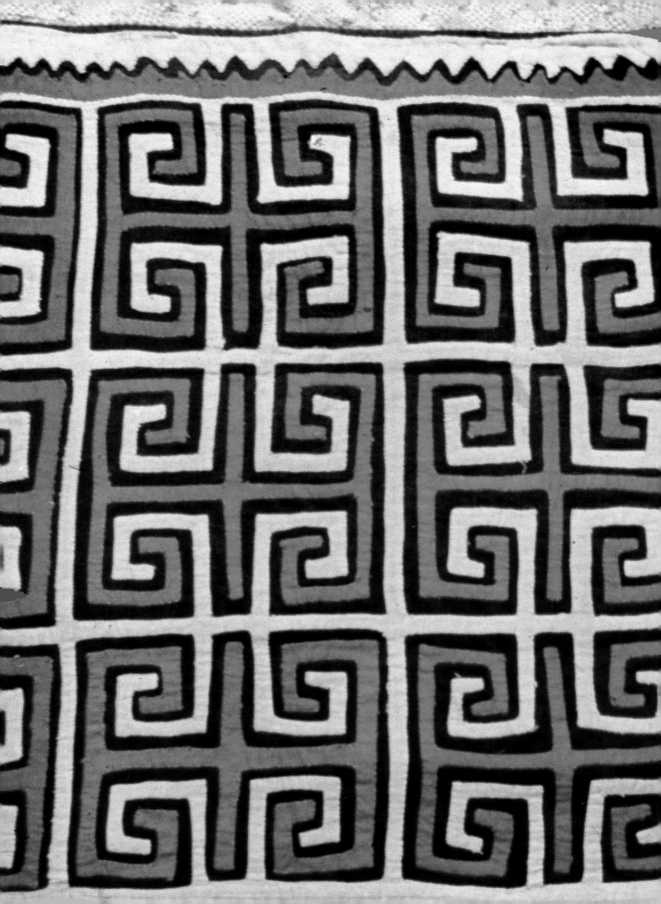

*Colour plate
corrugations*
See pages 208 and 209

Geometrical shapes derived from highly
stylised animals, plants and human
figures. Worked in four layers and using
the saw tooth edging throughout the
panel
British Museum, London

Mola with design similar to the hand
printed cotton skirt. This repetative
design is easy to enlarge in any direction
and could be used for any size figure
British Museum, London

The design of squirrels is fitted into a size
designed to fit the individual. It is
worked in five layers
British Museum, London

Unfinished mola panel. The zoomorphic
design is fitted into a panel of exact size.
A fifth layer would have to be added to
fill the large empty spaces between the
shapes to make it a serviceable garment
British Museum, London

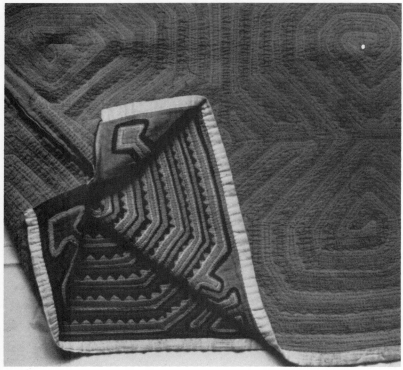

Both inside and outside of this mola with the spiral motif are qually beautiful. The inside layer has been joined to a piece of the same cotton fabric to give the required width to the blouse. The width of the fabric from selvage edge to selvage edge was often only 48·3 cm to 53·3 cm (19 in. to 21 in.) on the older molas

The main shape of the plant form of this mola exposes the dark bottom layer. This together with the many vertical cuts gives the panel a certain amount of stretch and elasticity and so makes a garment made from these panels more comfortable to wear

A mola made of two layers. The eyes of the chickens are worked on the lowest layer. They do not protrude above the general level of the embroidery

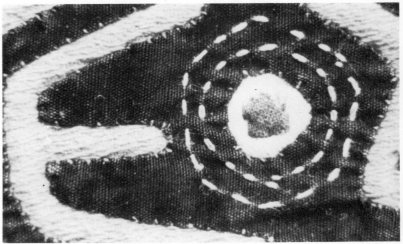

150

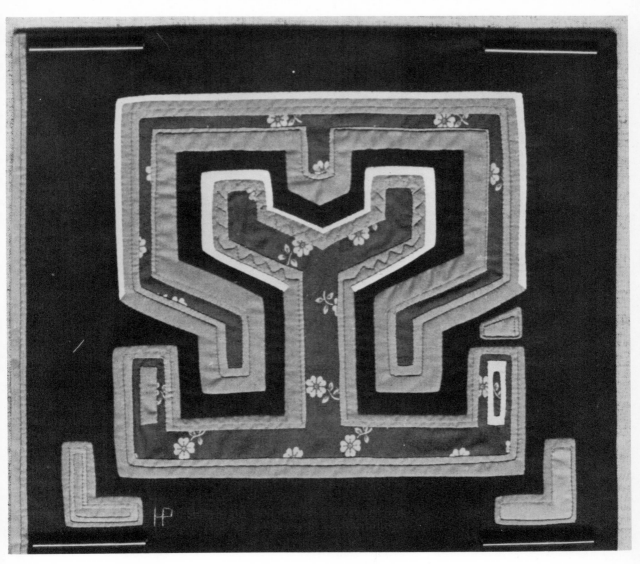

Small panels worked by children at school on the islands. A much more realistic approach shows the change and development of mola-making and the influence of tourists. These panels could not be made into garments. The craftsmanship is still superb

'Ailigandi' 35 cm × 33 cm (14 in. × 13 in.) Herta Puls. I used the Y-symbol for this panel based on the Ailigandi lectern fall on page 19 and built up from two basic layers by adding further layers in the way the Kuna Indians work. The Y-symbol had intrigued me all the time. It appears frequently on the molas and there seems to be no explanation of its significance

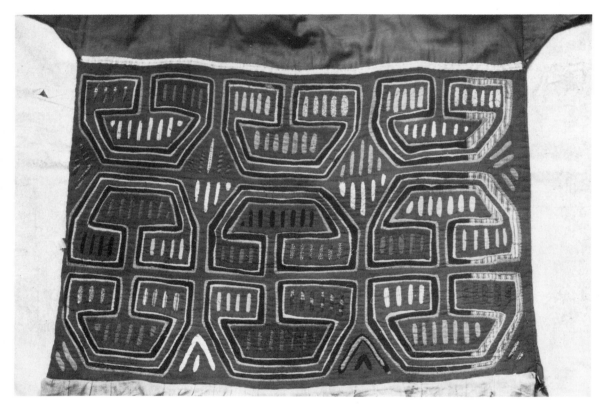

A mask mola

Working Methods for
Kuna Indian Appliqué

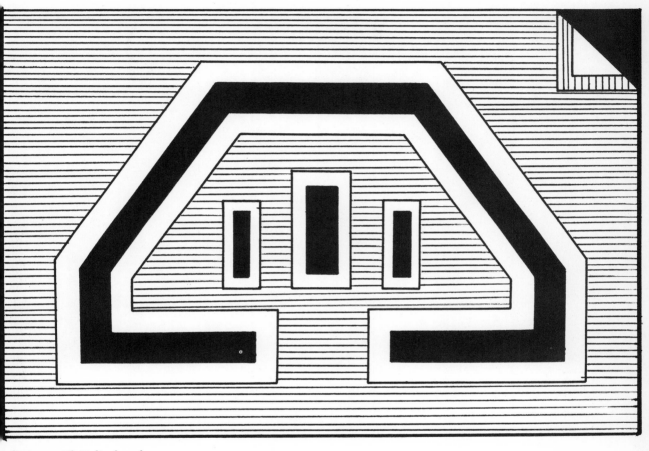

Design motif. Stylised mask

153

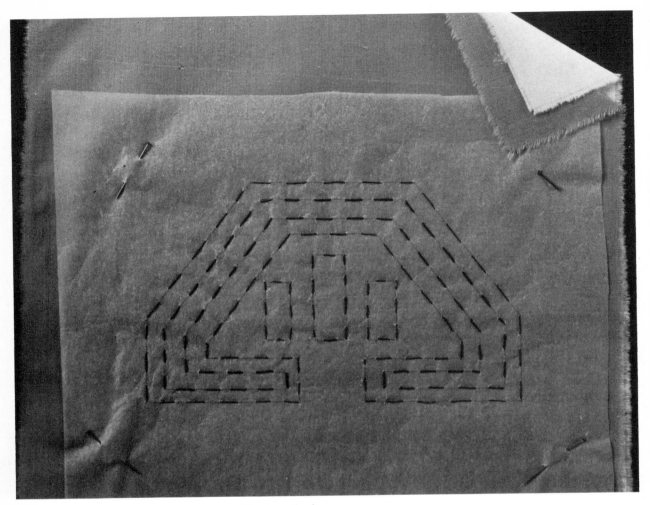

First method

From the drawing of the design make a transfer on greaseproof paper, **not** transfer paper, this is too thick. The design is to be worked in three layers. Take the three pieces of fabric and lay one on top of the other. Watch that the grain of each piece matches the grain of the other or lies at right angles to it. If this is not observed, unsightly puckering can occur. It is best to tear the cotton material for the panels, so that the straight grain can be seen easily. It is best, if the three pieces of fabric are of the same size. Also consider the effect of a light colour on top of a dark one. The dark colour may show through and so spoil the desired effect. Pin the transfer to the three layers and start tacking from the centre of the design with approximately 5 mm ($\frac{1}{4}$ in.) tacking stitches top and bottom on the design line, starting from the centre working outwards will help to keep the layers flat. Make sure corners are indicated. Start without knot, using single thread and stitch through all three layers of fabric and transfer.

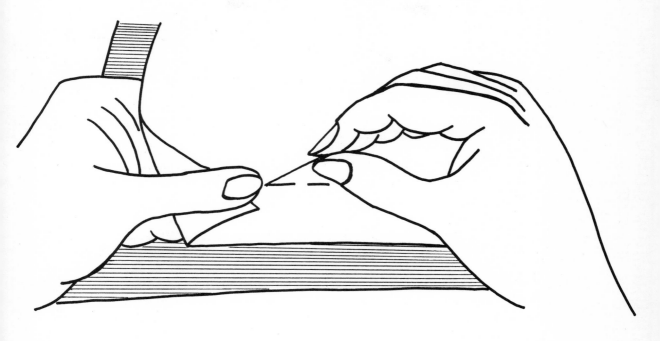

Take transfer off, by slicing with a pin or needle through the greaseproof paper where the tacking thread is on the SURFACE of the paper. Ease transfer off. It is best to rest the left hand on a firm surface, holding the transfer paper between fingers and thumb and gently easing the paper while cutting with the pin. The right hand should also be resting on the work, so that the transfer paper is held taut while the needle or pin slices through the paper. This produces a straight cut through which the tacking thread can slide.

The transfer is taken off in one piece by this method. It can be used for reference and later additions to the design can be transferred to the same piece of paper and added to the work. This is a clean and accurate method of transferring a design to fabric. It is advisable to use the same colour tacking thread for all design lines throughout the work to avoid confusion with other tacking lines. Run a rough tacking line, in a different colour, around the design about 10 mm–15 mm ($\frac{1}{2}$ in.–$\frac{3}{4}$ in.) away from the outside edge of the design. This prevents the layers of cloth from separating when cutting of the work starts. This line is shown on all the photographs.

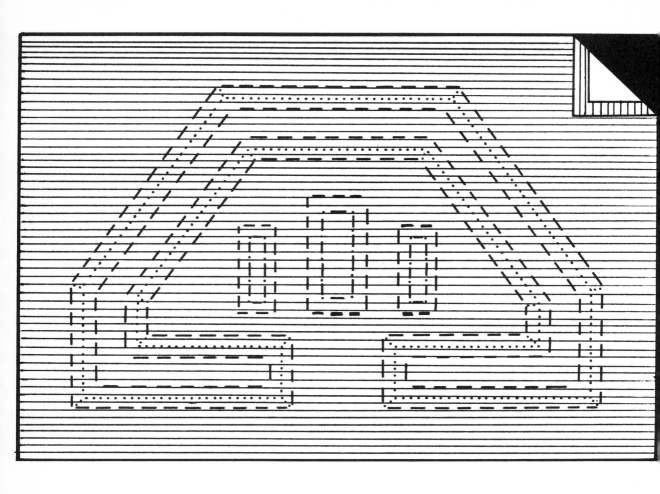

Cut through the top layer of the three pieces of fabric with sharp, pointed scissors about 5 cm (2 in.) at a time allowing for turnings. The dashed line on the drawing is the design line, the dotted line shows where to cut.

Snip design tacking threads where the layer has been cut. Carefully lift the top layer with the needle or scissors so that the tufts of the tacking thread stay in place on the next layer. With the edge which is to be worked horizontally, and the cut edge uppermost, start turning under the seam allowance from left to right using the needle to smooth the turning allowance until the folded edge lies on the tufts.

156

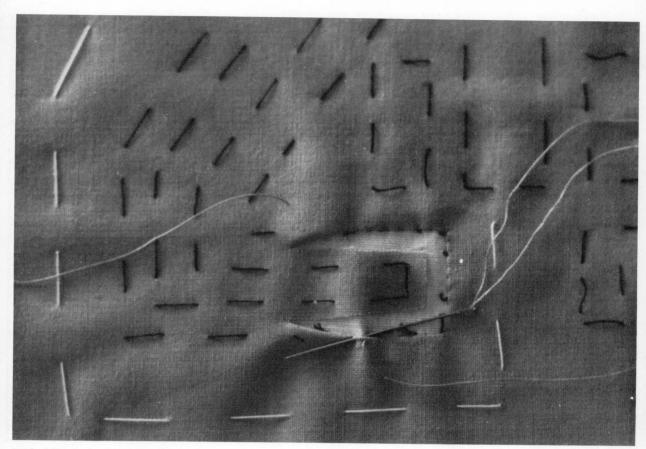

Dashed line is the design line for the first
and second layer. The stitched edge
shows the tufts of the design tacking and
the turned under edge with needle in
position for next stitch

Sew with small invisible hem-stitches with thread which matches
the colour of the top layer from right to left through all the three
layers. Continue until all the outer edges of the design have been
worked.

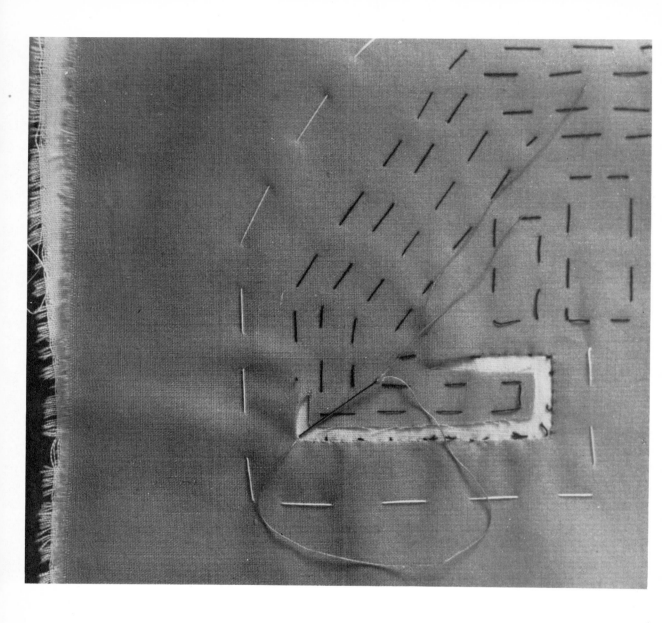

Needle in tabstitch position for the working of the corner. Bring the needle and thread up in the corner, through the top layer, angle the needle so that its point goes back into the same place but under the turning. The thread pulls the fabric to the point where the needle came up, so producing a sharp pointed corner.

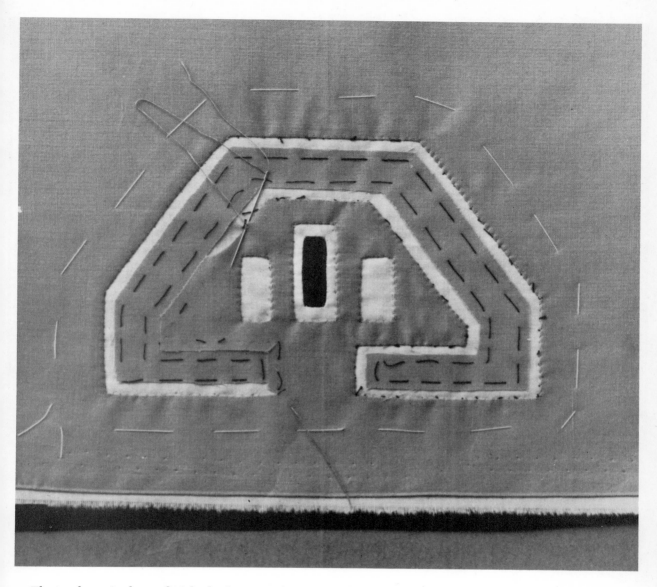

The top layer is almost finished. There are three centre rectangles. The two small rectangles were worked in the same way, in the middle one the next stage is completed. It also shows the design line for the second layer. Snip the design tacking threads for the second layer and carefully lift off the surplus fabric left from the top layer. This design line could now be re-tacked and the tufts removed from the back of the work.

The piece of fabric which is cut away between the lines of stitching can be left as one piece and can be used for another piece of work. This is the way the Kuna women make their molas. They use this cut away surplus piece often for the smaller shape of the same design on the second half of their mola blouse.

159

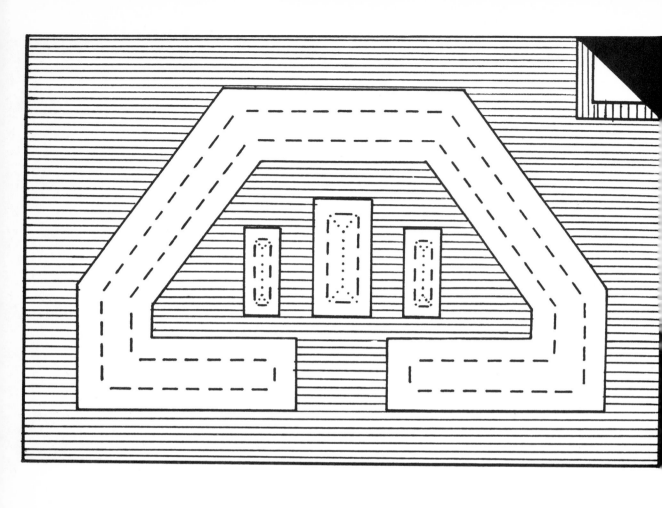

The solid line in the drawing is the finished top layer. The design line for the second layer is shown as a dashed line. The design lines have been re-tacked. The centre rectangles show the cutting line for the second layer as a dotted line.

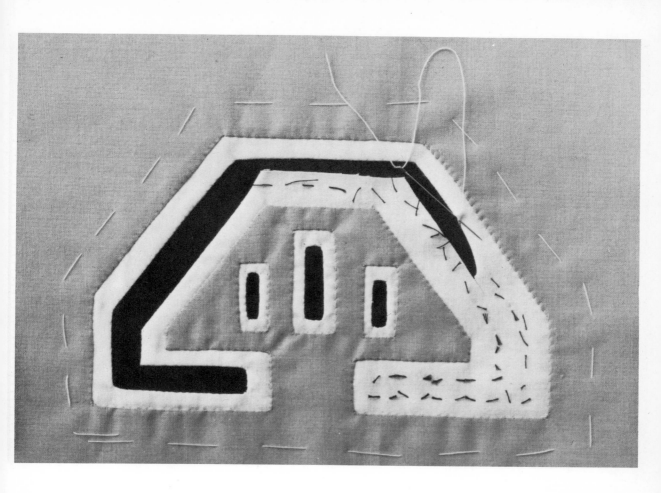

The top layer is finished. It shows where the second layer has been cut. The tufts are the snipped design line tacking threads for the second layer. The centre area is completed. The cutting line is halfway between the tacking lines in this example. When the second layer has been cut and worked with matching thread, the third layer is exposed (black).

The enlargement of part of the mask mola from page 15 (Symbols) shows the use of coloured printed fabric patches under the top layer

Transfer with two of the sides tacked.
The patch is being pushed into place
with the help of scissors

When working a design with a contrasting patch in the centre area start by pinning the design transfer on the three layers of fabric as before. Tack the design lines on two sides only. Cut a piece of contrasting or patterned material slightly smaller than the centre area of the design and slip it between top and second layer of fabric. The open side and base should make this possible. Finish tacking the transfer to the three layers, four layers in the centre.

Now proceed as before and the result will be as shown on page 164.

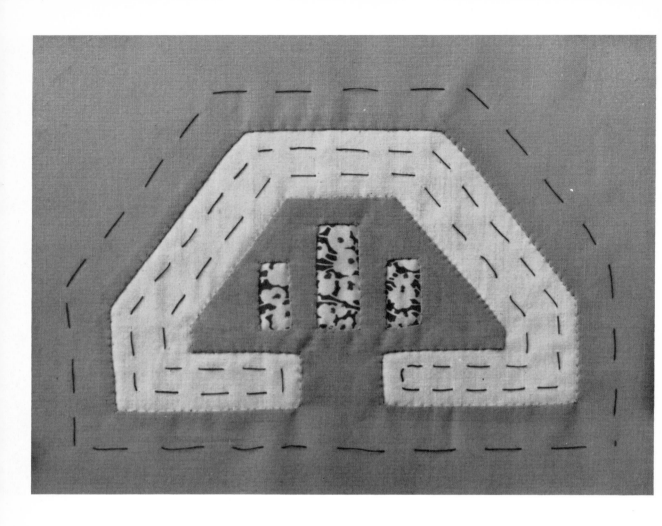

All the top layer has been worked and the design line for the next layer has been re-tacked. Centre rectangles with coloured patterned patch are finished. The patterned centre rectangles can be left or cut again to expose the original second layer.

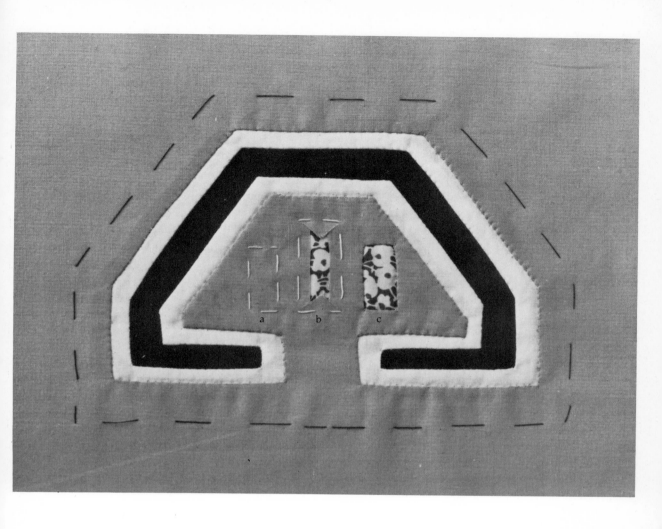

Top and second layer of main part have been worked. The centre rectangles were (a) tacked, (b) cut and (c) worked after the main part was finished. A much better way of inserting and working contrasting patches will be described in the second method. The working process of this method can be used with four or five layers of fabric, provided the distance between the original design lines is wide enough to allow more cutting and turning of seam allowances after two layers have been cut and worked.

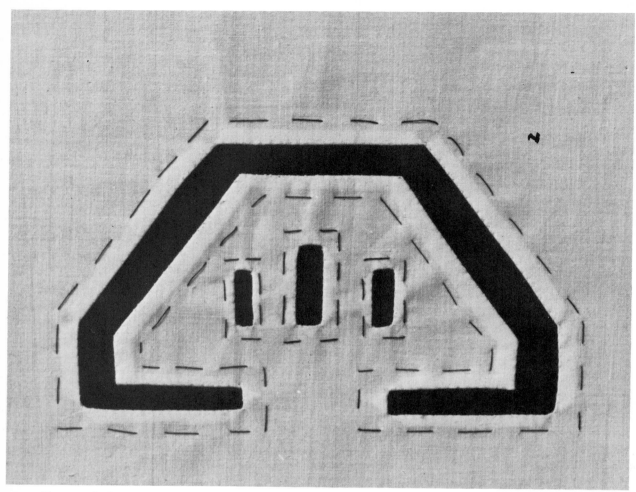

Second layer applied, the dashed line is the design line for the top layer. This design line secures the two layers of fabric and it is not necessary to run a rough tacking line around the design on the two layers, as was necessary in the first method

The second method is worked by starting with two layers of fabric and adding layers one by one until the top layer is added last. Instead of cutting and applying the top layer first, the second layer is applied to the base layer first. Pin the design transfer to the base and second layer of fabric watching that the grain of the two fabrics lies in the same direction. Tack the design transfer to the two layers as described in the first method. Remove transfer as in the first method and snip design line tacking for second layer. Start to cut, not forgetting the seam allowance, turn under the seam allowance to the tufts of the design line and stitch with thread matching second layer. The second layer now covers the work except for the area where the third or base layer is exposed.

166

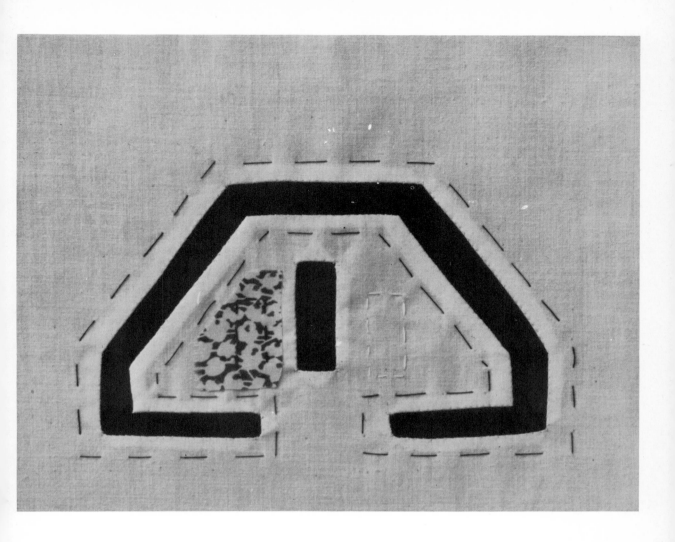

A contrasting patterned patch has been tacked on the two layers
on the design lines for the left-hand rectangle. The design lines for
the patch were tacked from the back the work. The middle
shape has been cut and stitched to the base, the right-hand shape
shows only the design tacking line. A patch could be cut to cover
this or a patch could be cut to cover the three rectangles. Differently
coloured or patterned patches could be added or applied on this
layer around the outside of the design. The dashed line is the design
line for the top layer.

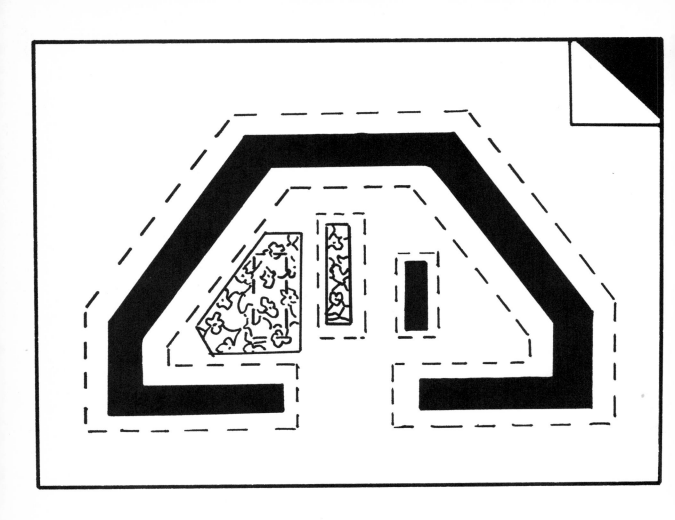

The drawing shows a contrasting patch tacked to the two layers as in the photograph on page 167, the right-hand side shape and outer design area have been worked, showing the base layer. The middle shape represents a trimmed patch with turned under seam allowance which has been stitched to the second layer on the design line (appliquéd). The dashed line surrounding it is the design line for the top layer. The top or third layer can now be added.

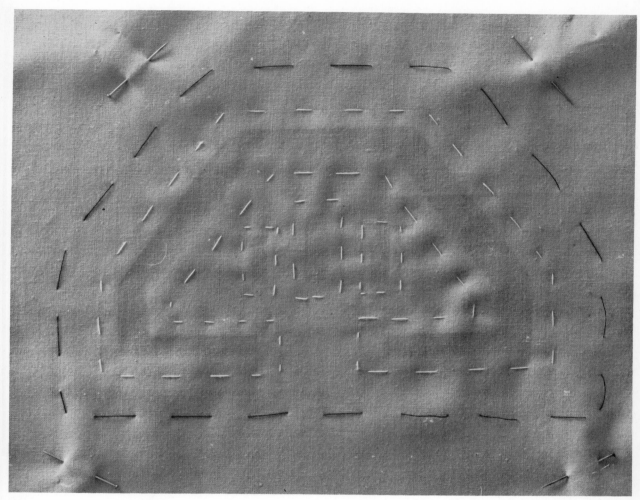

The third layer has been pinned to the completed two layers. The dashed white lines are the design tacking lines, the dashed black line is the rough tacking line

Pin piece of fabric to the completed two layers, watching again that the grain lies in the right direction. Turn the work over and on the tacking lines visible at the back tack the three pieces of cloth together, starting with the centre area. Work a rough tacking line around the design, about 10 mm–15 mm ($\frac{1}{2}$ in.–$\frac{3}{4}$ in.) away from the outer design tacking line.

The reverse side of the work. On the reverse side the previous stitching line and the design tacking line can be clearly seen.

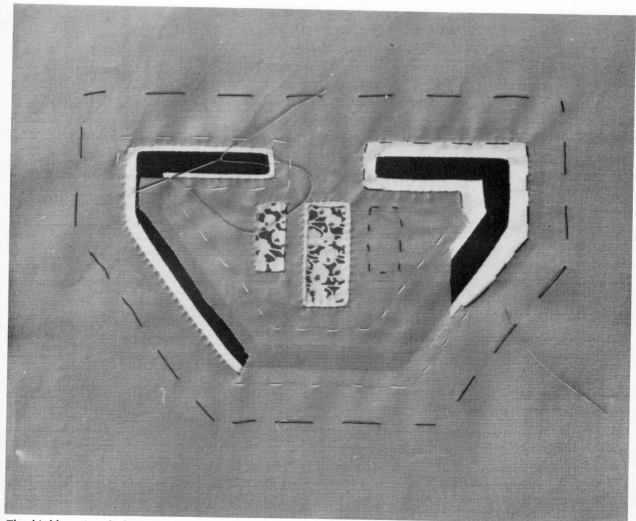

The third layer is tacked, cut and partially worked. In the centre area the middle rectangle has been worked as described on page 168 and the top layer stitched around it with a very narrow margin of the second layer exposed. The rough tacking line around the design holds the three layers together.

The stitching line on the previous layer can be seen through the covering layer. This line is the guide for cutting the top layer. When using a dark or thicker fabric this guiding line or ridge has to be felt before cutting

Now start cutting, allowing for turnings. Snip the tacking stitches and lift the edge for turning. This will reveal the original design tacking line on the second layer of the work.

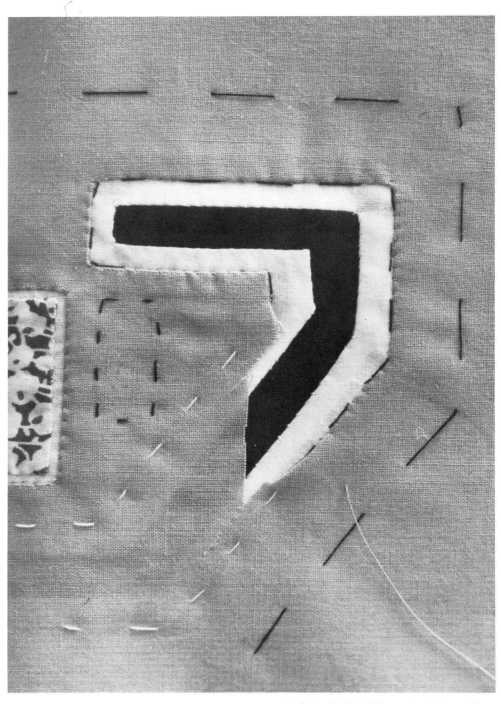

Left-hand side of the work. It shows the exposed original design line on the second layer, the tacking line which holds the three layers together and the finished part of the base and second layer

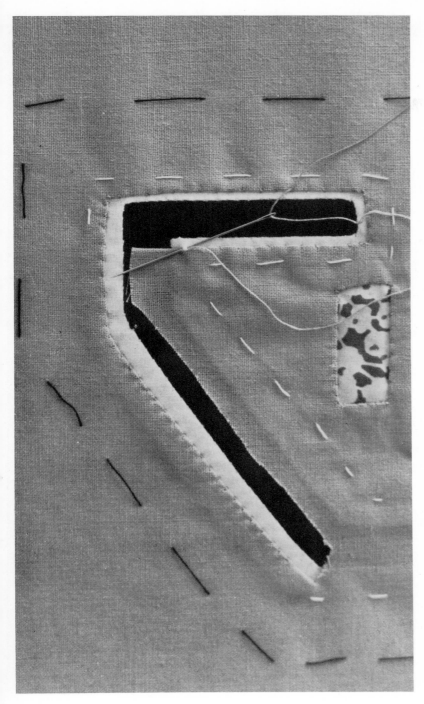

The right-hand side of the work with only half the seam allowance turned under and stitched. This shows, that with the second method it is possible to get very narrow margins around a shape, as can also be seen on pages 171 and 172, around the centre rectangle. This is impossible with the first method I have described. The needle is shown in the right position for working the corner. The seam allowance will have to be trimmed and turned under to the point where the needle last appeared on the surface of the work to ensure a perfect corner

Completed piece of work

The finished work in this example will look exactly like the design drawing when worked without the contrasting patches which ever method is used. More layers could now be added by the same process and by working lines parallel to the existing ones. New design features can be added to the original drawing, traced on the design transfer and tacked to the piece of work on any layer. They could either be achieved by a patch of fabric which is covered by the next layer, or by a feature which is first worked and then cut back to, on the subsequent layer. With both methods it is possible to add layers and patches to the back of the work. This is not advisable for articles which are going to be worn, as the patches would fray and look untidy and the extra layer would not have enough stitches to hold them in place. The Kuna mola has the patches always sandwiched between layers, sometimes a whole layer is made up from many different patches. They do not use many tacking lines, only enough to keep the larger shapes in place. After stitching these shapes and may be adding patches by tacking, they feel the stitched edges and work freely as their imagination inspires them.

A mola is never lined. With very flimsy materials the base layer is worked with another layer as one. I have seen many molas where the quilted appearance of the reverse side was almost as beautiful as

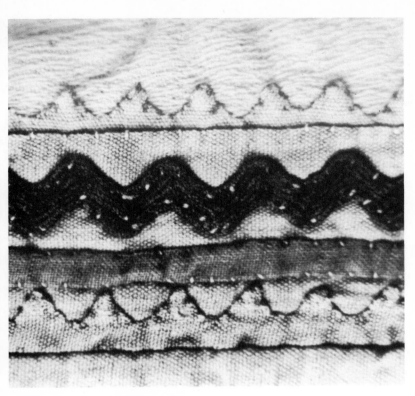

Combination of stitched zigzag edging
and rick-rack braid

the outside. In fashioning the front and back of her mola, the Kuna woman often uses the larger cut out shapes of the one side for the slightly smaller ones on the other.

I hope that from the description of the two working methods it is quite apparent that the technique is pure cut work and appliqué. The term 'reverse appliqué', which is often used, is to my mind quite out of place.

On many of the oldest molas and some of the modern ones the shapes or part of the shapes are worked with a zigzag edging, sometimes called saw-tooth edge. This line also appears in the Kuna picture writing surrounding a symbol and represents there the umbilical cord which is of great importance in the Kuna mythology of creation.

The working of the zigzag or saw-tooth edging, on a straight edge. Trim the seam allowance to just above the design line. The points of the triangles or 'teeth' will finish on the design line. Then make straight cuts at regular intervals at right angles to the design line. The length of these cuts will determine the height of the triangles, the distance between the cuts the width at the base of the triangle. From the centre of the fabric between the two cuts turn under one corner (right hand) with the needle, smooth down and stitch with matching thread. The triangles are worked from right to left with the cut edge uppermost. Bring out the needle at the point of the triangle just below the top, then turn under the second corner. Make one stitch at the top of the point and stitch to the bottom of the second side of the triangle.

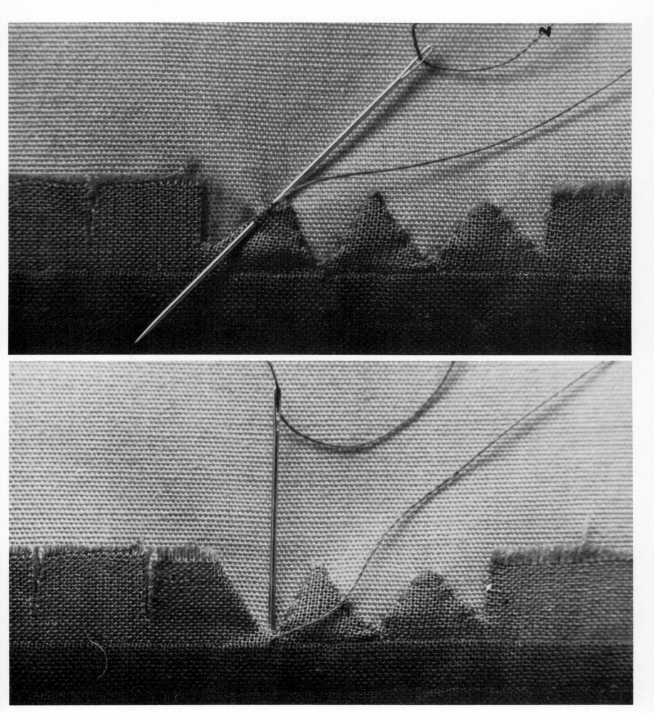

Stitch down the second side of the triangle. From the centre of
the next section turn down corner. Make one stitch between
triangles and work one side up as on first triangle. Continue until
all triangles have been worked.

177

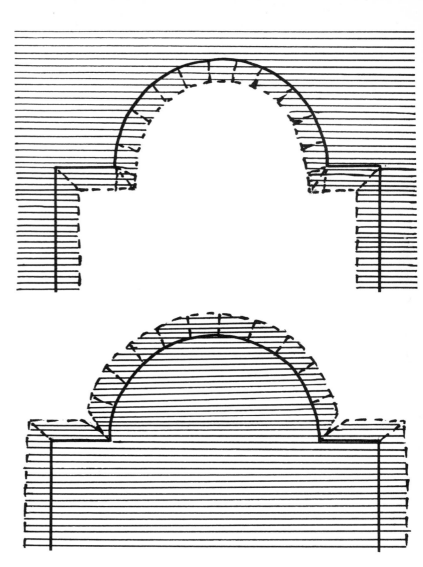

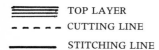

TOP LAYER
CUTTING LINE
STITCHING LINE

Working the zigzag edge on a curved line. On a curved edge the cuts have to be slanted. The cut must be at right angles to the base of the triangle.

Right-angle corners on a piece of work present a difficulty. The cuts have to be carefully planned and placed, so that there is a triangle on either side of the corner or one across the corner.

If a zigzag line is required below the top layer in working the first method, the length of the cut is limited by the stitching line of the top layer. The cut must not touch this stitching line. Enough fabric must remain to accommodate the turning of the corner. In the second method the layer covering the layer with the finished zigzag edge can be worked so that either only the points of the triangles show or the complete triangle with some of the layer they are worked on.

178

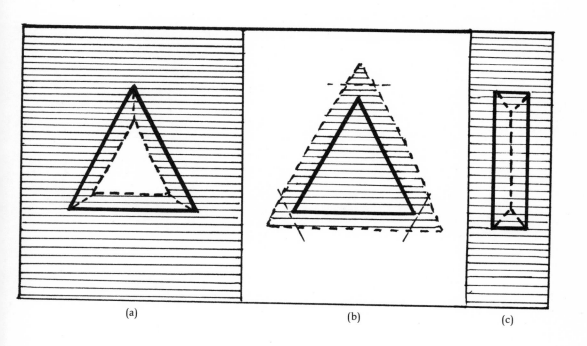

(a)   (b)   (c)

The process of snipping the seam allowance on a curved edge applies to all appliqué work to enable the material to lie flat. Always cut at right angles to the design line.

Pointed shapes are easier to work when the turning allowance is on the inner edge of the shape. Figure (a).

If the turning allowance is on the outer edge the points need to be trimmed as in figure (b).

For a narrow slit cut as in figure (c).

179

Kuna Molas selected for their artistic merit

The photographs on the following pages show not only the technical skill but also the high artistic quality which some of the women have achieved in the design of their molas.

Colour is an essential ingredient of mola art, without it the full impact cannot be appreciated. The black and white illustrations at least show the considerable talent of the Kuna women for formal arrangement. Unless otherwise stated the molas are from the author's collection.

Facing page
Kuna Woman from the Karti group of the San Blas Islands sewing her mola

181

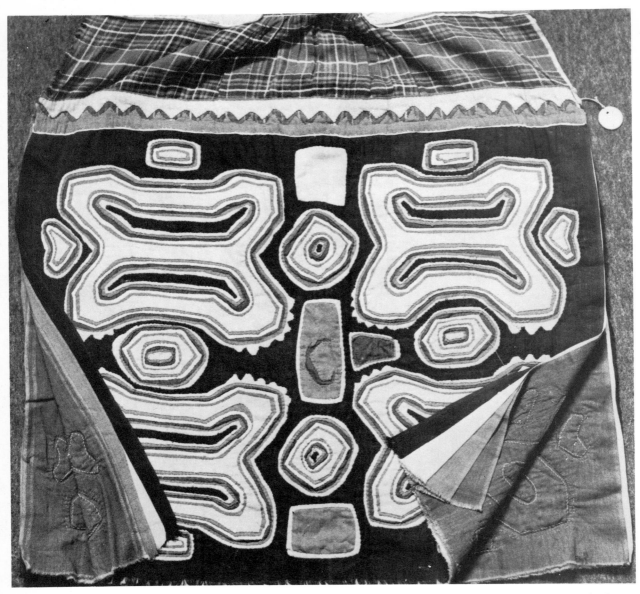

Unfinished mola panel showing the four
layers of fabric which make up this panel
British Museum, London

Mola with bird and dog pattern from
Achutupu (Dog island)

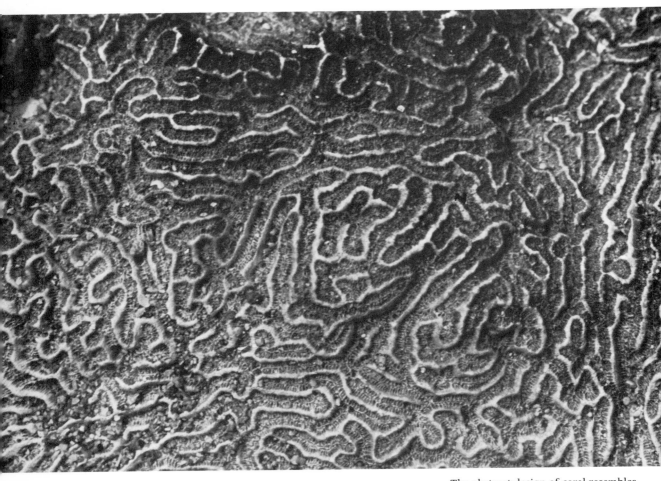

The abstract design of coral resembles
many of the mola designs

Abstract design on an old mola
British Museum, London

Enlarged photograph of brain-cor.

Facing page

Events in Kuna life lead to mola making
of high artistic quality. Probably incense
burners used at religious ceremonies

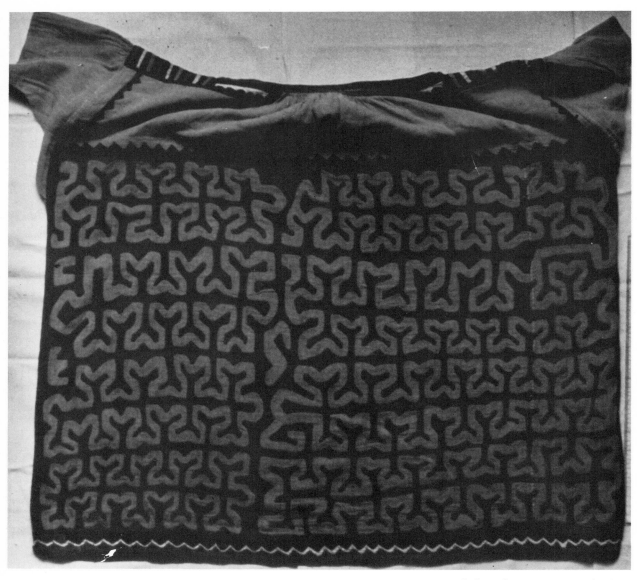

Mola from the Rio Caiman, Colombia
Ethnographic Museum, Gothenburg

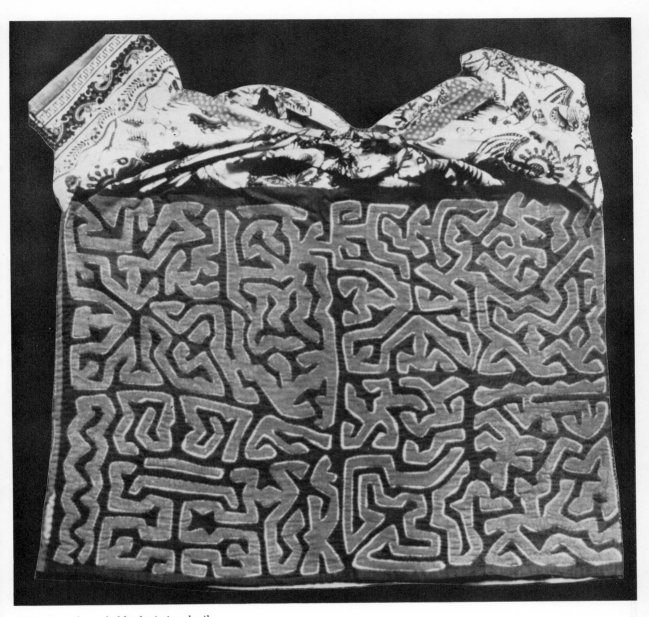

Abstract mola probably depicting devils,
collected in 1920. See also colour plate
facing page 120
Ethnographic Museum, Gothenburg

Mola based on bird on lizard from the
collection of Lady Richmond Brown
British Museum, London

Modern mola in two colours

The life of the sea surrounding them influenced many of their designs

Modern lobster-scorpion mola

Modern geometric design. See also colour plate facing page 121

The geometric design on this old mola is
still being used on modern molas
British Museum, London

The oldest mola in the Gothenburg
Museum collected in 1912

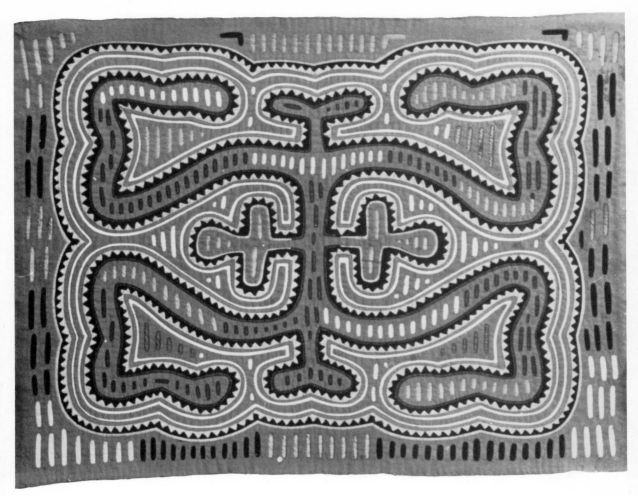

A modern mola

A modern story telling mola. Catching a saw-fish

Monsters, probably evil spirits, a recent
mola

Abstract design, motivated by steam
boats
British Museum, London

Kuna Woman from Ailigandi

Fossil

A personal approach

My belief is that all works of art relate in some way to the order which exists in nature. The artist's ability to embrace the environment, which includes religious and moral beliefs as well as outside influences, enables him to observe everything around him with an open mind. With his special awareness he collects and sorts information from his own group but also from influences outside his own circle, moulds them into a unity and translates them into imagery with which we can identify. Not only the artist but also the object he is interested in depends on the environment. These relationships must be realised, sorted and assembled to a unique personal statement, whether in visual art or music or literature.

I have been so impressed by the Kuna Indians, not only by their embroidery but also by their philosophy and the way in which they have come to terms with their environment, that it has had considerable influence on my own judgement of western standards and with that on my work. I began by using layers of cotton fabric stretched tightly in a frame and working from designs which were inspired by fine detail in natural structures. I am often surprised and delighted when looking at quite ordinary objects, how nature's design is beautiful and functional to the smallest detail and how subtle its colours and shapes are. The smooth flat texture and soft colouring of the cotton gave unity to the work and seemed very suited to the designs. After working several panels in this way, I began to feel a need for the softness and the flexibility of the textile to be incorporated in the work. This feeling became very strong after my visit to the Kuna Indians on their islands and seeing the women stitch during every spare minute, with their work on their lap, rolling it up when duty called and going back to it at the first opportunity. I also wanted to use some stitches to achieve some texture in the smooth shapes of cotton.

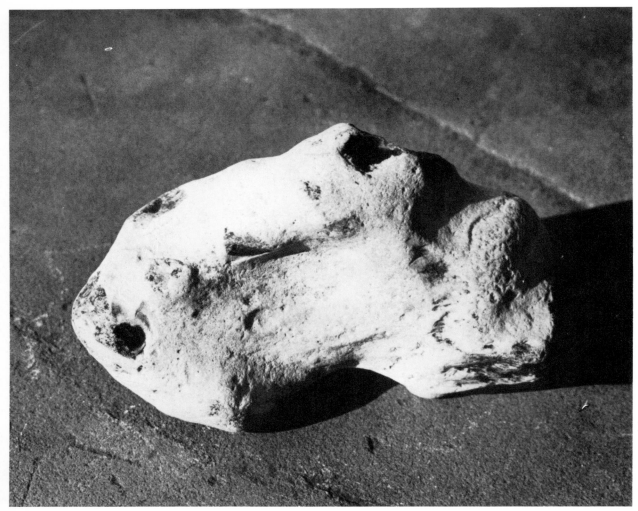

Stone

204

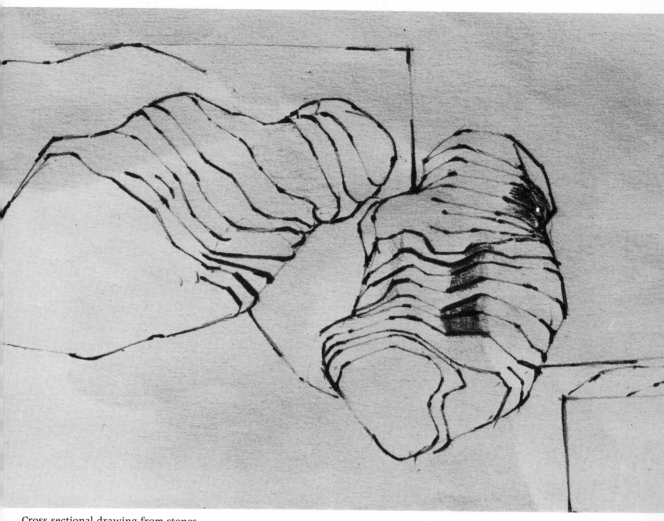

Cross sectional drawing from stones

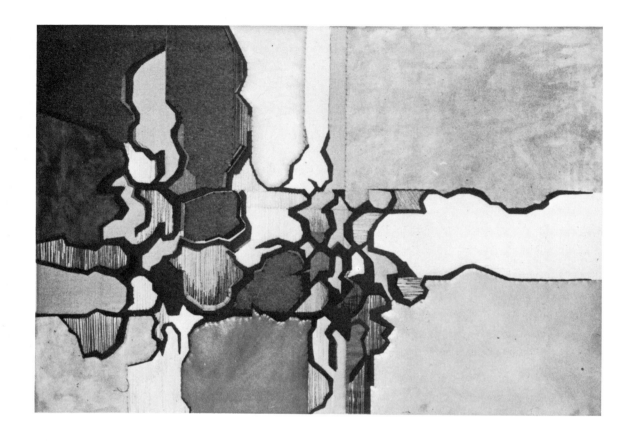

Flintstones were a source of inspiration and information. Touching the stones and feeling their form made me aware of the changes of planes and led to a series of analytical drawings of cross sections which produced interesting linear rhythms and irregular shapes between the lines. I used these for the panel *Flint* (33 cm × 77 cm (23 in. × 33½ in.). The top layer of this piece of work is dark brown felt, with shapes of leather and suede in natural to brown colours applied afterwards.

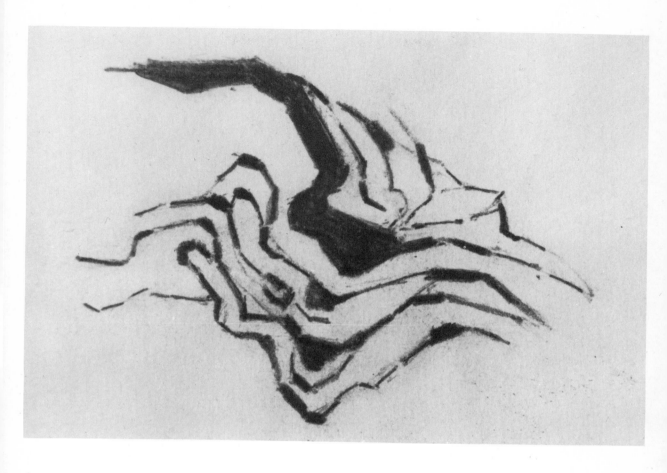

I was particularly intrigued by the exquisite curves and ridges and colours of a shrivelled pear which, left in a drawer and forgotten, had almost mummified. I used drawings from this for a number of panels. Although the object was different and the shapes and contours analysed from a different point of view, the created images were not dissimilar to my drawings from flint stones. This happens all the time when drawing forms from nature, it becomes clear that all organic shapes conform to certain proportions and shape characteristics. My analytical studies are always carried out in broad media like charcoal or chalk. This leads to a stronger and broader approach.

Drawing

From the objective study of a fragment of the surface of the pear, a subjective drawing evolved, creating a greater feeling of the organic movements of the structure. All organic forms are in fact built from curves.

Facing page
Corrugations   The panel was worked on fine cotton needlecord with layers of plain cotton poplin, felt and leather. The shapes spread into the suede frame which was again framed by a second suede frame. The padded effect is a result of the built up layers. 62·5 × 100 cm (25 × 40 in.). See also colour plate facing page 145.

209

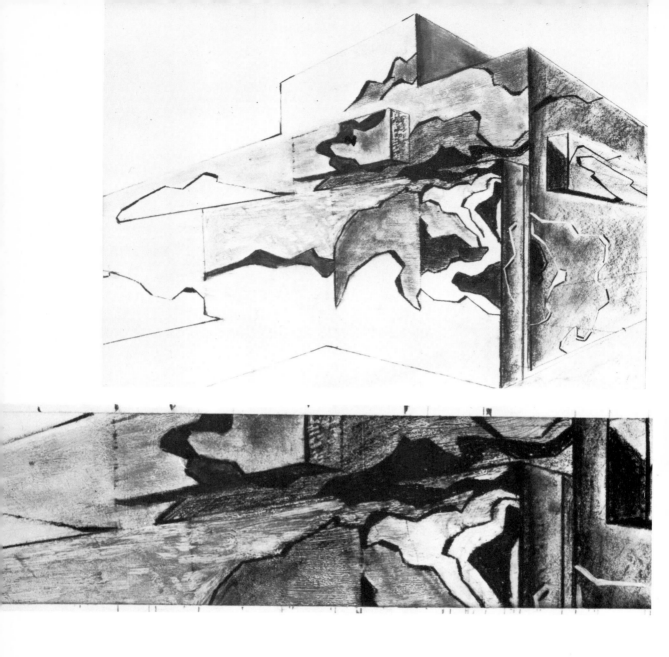

One set of analytical drawings can be the foundation for a number of ideas. In the first drawing the visual information from the pear is related to a perspective structure. From this a detail was selected and re-drawn.

Illusion 87·6 cm × 61 cm (34½ in. × 24 in.)

The central section of the piece of embroidery on this page is developed from the detail seen on the previous page. The surrounding frame is based on the special illusion which perspective creates. The colour in this work is based on the low keyed colours discovered in my first analysis of the pear. The centre piece is worked in plain cotton poplins. The frame in sections covered with organdie, cotton, suede and leather.

Sea shell. The shapes formed by cross sections of the sea shell became the Chinese symbol Yang-Yin, where the light shape represented male and the dark shape female. It was also a symbol of pre-Columbian cultures in South America.

In these studies from the sea shell I became more and more aware of the implications of the spiral and the concave and convex character of the shapes which produce a strong effect of light and shade. At this point I felt the need to create three dimensional form. I explored the previously mentioned characteristics by carving into a block of plaster of Paris and creating a form which bears little relationship to the appearance of the sea shell but incorporates the nature of the shapes and their rhythm.

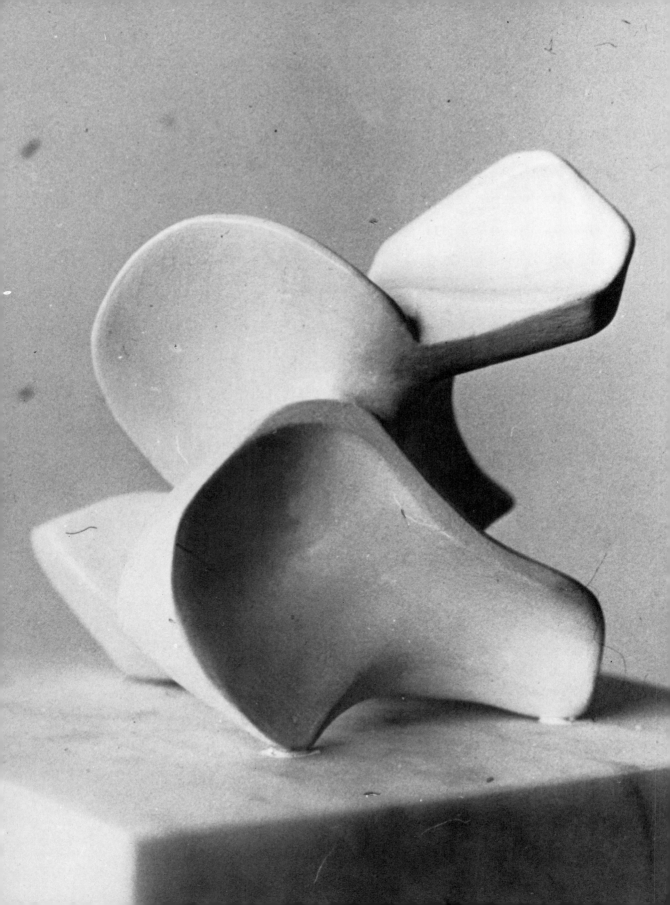

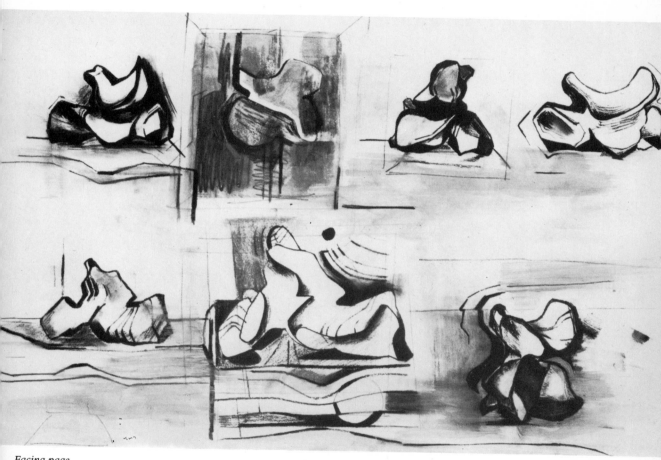

Facing page
Sculptured form derived from sea shell

Sheet of studies showing sculptured form
seen from various angles

A selection of shapes
from the study sheet
drawn onto lino and cut.
Reverse side. One block
stained

216

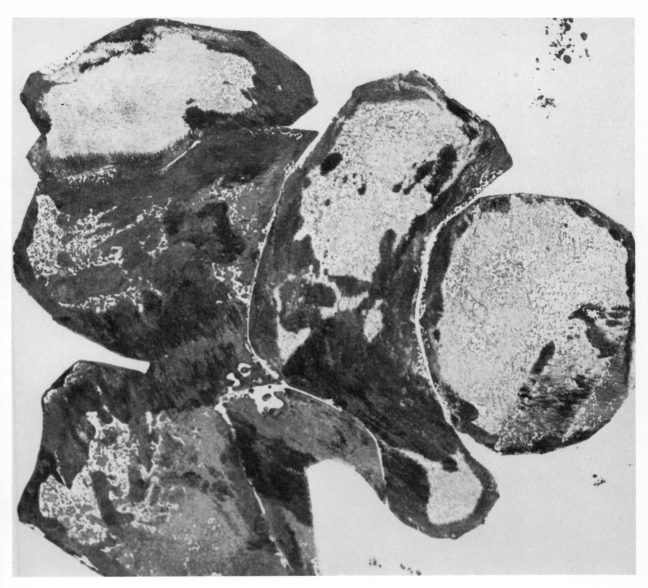

Lino print

Overleaf
One of the prints which did not follow the original form was the
starting point for the finished piece of embroidery.

Cuna Shell
This was worked in 3 layers of cotton poplin. The bottom layer of
brushed denim was embroidered to create texture. The hanging is
43·2 cm ×× 61 cm (17 in. × 24 in.).

There are many other stages of the development of an idea which
have not been illustrated. In my opinion all worthwhile ideas go
through many stages before the final idea is resolved.

217

Lino print with drawn and painted
surround

218

Cuna Shell

Photograph of bark

Study sheet of drawings from bark

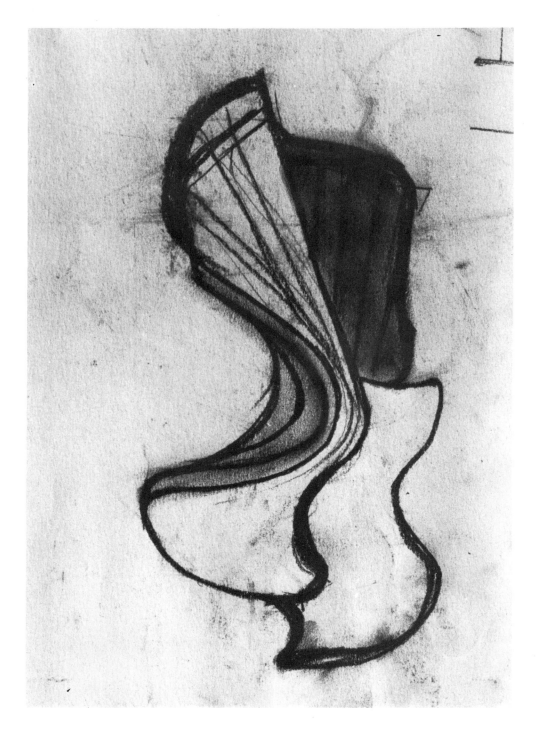

Detail from first study sheet re-drawn at a larger scale. This became the starting point for the next development, which was to carve an image in plaster of Paris based on the drawing.

Three dimensional plaster form

At this stage I had no clear conception of the way the final design would evolve.

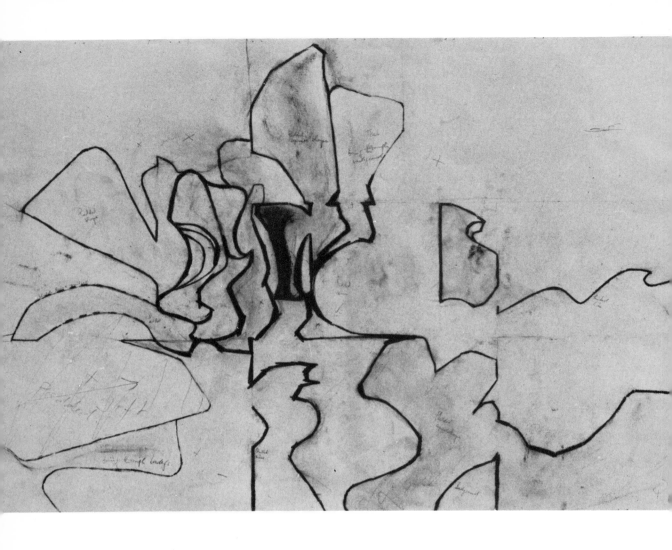

I subdivided a sheet of paper into an asymmetrical rectangular grid, keeping a balanced relation of the sections. Into one of these units I placed the three dimensional form which was flat on one side, and developed my design around it, echoing in various ways the shapes already clearly defined in the plaster.

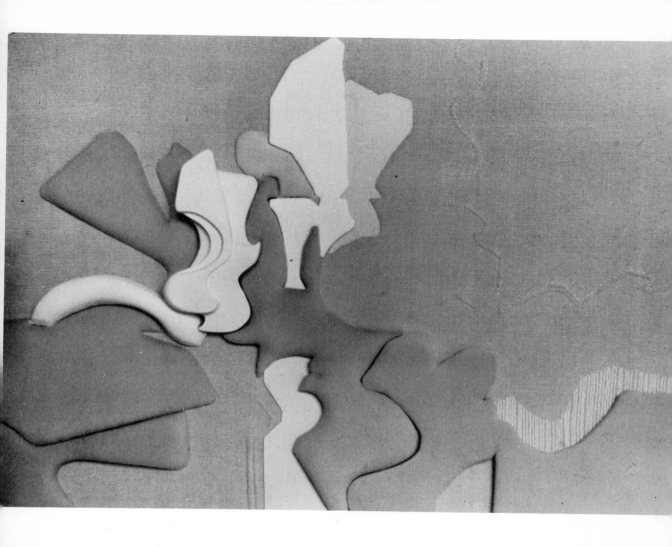

Finished piece of work *Metamorphosis* 77·3 cm × 62.2 cm (34½ in. × 24½ in.). In the finished piece of work the plaster form became the focal point. The padded areas around were gradually reduced in height and softened in substance, back to the two-dimensional surface of the panel. The whiteness of the plaster inspired the colours, which were subtle graduations from white to a deepish creamy-grey colour. The materials used were knitted brushed nylon, an evenweave woollen base mounted on calico and white glacé kid.

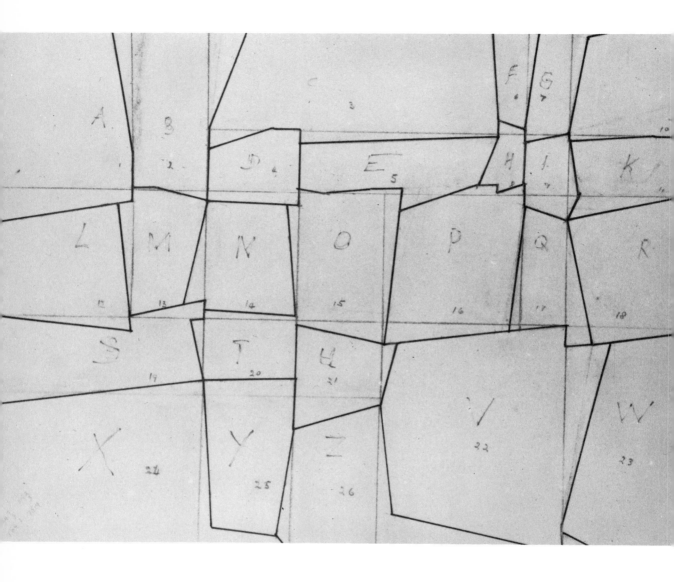

A way of achieving a large panel was by working each detail separately. I have always liked the shapes of letters in their different execution, not as something one can read, but as a design achieved by using their shapes. This I admired in the molas, where the women use letters, which are without meaning to them, just as shapes.

The start for my panel A–Z was a grid of 26 spaces. To make it more interesting I slightly altered the angles of the dividing lines and offset the joins.

I then fitted shapes of letters into the so created spaces.

228

Finished hanging A–Z. The cotton fabric I used was arranged in the same sequence of three colours, black, orange, red for each letter. I worked on two layers, black and orange first, only changing the colour of each actual letter by either cutting back or by removing the negative shape around it. I then added the red layer. The top layer was one piece of blue cotton 135 cm × 120 cm (54 in. × 48 in.) into which the letters were set.

An example where I used the letters of the word TEN is 'Cuna Ten'. Design collage. The design was fitted into a space 25 cm (10 in.) square. It was worked in three colours of plain cotton poplin.

The embroidery became the base of the piece of work. Above this base I erected a triangular frame which consisted of a piece of perspex 25 cm × 52 cm (10 in. × 20¼ in.) bent in the middle to produce two 25 cm (10 in.) squares. These fitted exactly over the mounted piece of work, the ridge being the apex of a triangular cross section. Each square had a square of perspex removed to leave a framework of 19 mm (¾ in.) wide. Over this framework I wrapped ten sections of fine sewing cotton over each square. Through this filter the cutwork could be seen. This superimposing of colours produced a change in the visual appearance of the embroidered base.

'Cuna Ten'

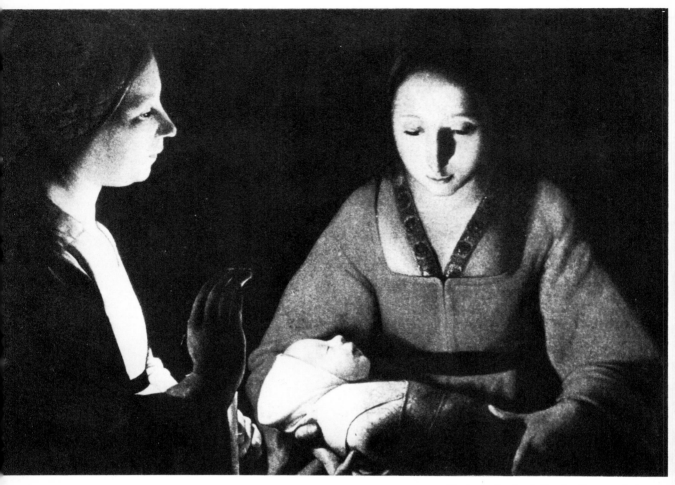

Photograph of painting by Georges de la Tour *Newborn Babe*. Seventeenth century

Facing page
Transcription in pencil. I selected a detail from the painting and drew this in pencil, being careful to retain original proportions. Then using a technical device from television of lines running parallel but using the lines diagonally, I achieved the sensation of light and flicker of the image by lightening and darkening these and using broad and narrow sections.

234

Facing page
The finished embroidery *Fragments* was worked in tones of brown and black on two layers of white organdie. The transparent embroidery stressed the contrast of solid lines which were worked in stitches and applied leather and suede. 50 cm × 56 cm (22 in. × 22 in.).

The detail shows in greater clarity the materials.

Technical information

Stitches used for cutwork

Running stitch	For all types of outlining and quilting
Overcasting	In broderie Anglaise used for eyelet holes
Blanket stitch **Buttonhole stitch**	For all cutwork
Buttonhole stitch bars with picots	Used in Richelieu work and Venetian cutwork
Buttonhole fillings	Used in Italian cutwork and Hedebo embroidery, resembling Reticella lace
Chain stitch	Used in outlining Dresden work shapes and for padding of raised cutwork (Venetian)
Chain stitch combined with double lines of running stitch	Also used for padding of raised cutwork (Venetian work)
Darning stitch	Running stitch which picks up and covers precise number of threads and creates a woven fabric when completed. The same stitch is used for needleweaving on the bars in cutwork. (Hardanger work, Richelieu work – with or without picots – and in Venetian work)
Satin stitch	A flat stitch which is used for surface embroidery, for Kloster blocks in Hardanger embroidery, for Hedebo embroidery and Algerian eye stitch
Faggot stitch	For creating open net ground as in Russian ground
Stem stitch	Used to outline eyelet holes in broderie Anglaise and Madeira work and for surface stitchery
French knots and Bullion knots	For surface embroidery on all cut work

Stitches used in appliqué

Hem stitch	For attaching one fabric to another
Blind hem stitch **Buttonhole stitch** **Blanket stitch** **Herringbone stitch**	Also for applying fabrics
Overcasting	For applying or couching threads and finishing edges
Running stitch	For tacking patches or transferring patterns to fabrics. For quilting patchwork or quilting between applied pieces of fabric, for surface stitchery around applied patches, see Kuna embroidery
Chain stitch	For applying patches or for surface embroidery around and on applied work
French knots and Bullion knots	For surface embroidery
Couching	Applying thread or cord to fabric by oversewing

Bibliography

ABBOT, WILLIS J: *Panama and the Canal*, Dodd, Mead & Co, 1914

ANTON, FERDINAND: *Art of the Maya*, Thames & Hudson, London, 1968

ANTON, FERDINAND and DOCKSTADER, FREDERICK: *Pre-Colombian Art*, Harry N Abrams, New York/London

BELL, ELEANOR Y: *Republique of Panama and its People*, Annual Report, Smithsonian Institution, Washington, DC, 1909

BROWN, LADY RICHMOND: *Unknown Tribes Uncharted Seas*, Duckworth, 1924

DOCKSTADER, FREDERICK: *Indian Art of Central America*, Cory Adams & Mackay

EDWARDS, JOAN: *Crewel Embroidery in England*, Batsford, 1975

ESQUEMELING: *The Buccaneers of America*, originally printed in English for William Crooke, London, 1684

FEENEY, CORINNE B: *Arch Isolationists, the San Blas Indians*, National Geographic Magazine, Vol. 79, No. 2, 1941

FINLEY, RUTH E: *Old Patchwork Quilts and the Women who made them*, Grosset & Dunlap, New York, 1929

HABERLAND, WOLFGANG: *Gold in Alt-Amerika*, Hamburgisches Museum für Völkerkunde, 1972; *Zentral Mexico*, ditto, 1974

HOLMER, NILS M: *Ethno-Linguistic Cuna Dictionary*, Gothenburg, 1952

JELLIFFE, D B, et al: *The Children of the San Blas Indians*, Tropical Pediatrics, Vol. 59, August 1961

KEELER, CLYDE E: *Cuna Indian Art*, Exposition Press, New York, 1969

KELLY, JOANNE M: *Cuna*, A S Barnes & Co Inc, South Brunswick, NY, 1966

KÖHLER, CARL: *A History of Costume*, Dover Publications, New York, 1963

KRIEGER, HERBERT: *Material Culture of the People of South Eastern Panama*, Bulletin 134, United States National Museum, Washington, DC, 1926

LOTHROP, SAMUEL K, et al: *Coclé, an Archeological Study of Central Panama*, Memoirs of the Peabody Museum of Archeology and Ethnology, Harvard University, Vol. 7, 1937

LOTHROP, SAMUEL K: *Essays in Pre-Colombian Art and Archeology*, Harvard University Press, 1961

LOTHROP, SAMUEL K: *Treasures of Ancient America*, Institute of Andean Research, 1964

MACKENZIE, DONALD A: *The Migration of Symbols*, Kegan Paul, Trench, Turner & Co Ltd, London, 1926

MCKIM, FRED: *San Blas, An Account of the Cuna Indians of Panama; The Forbidden Land, Reconnaissance of Upper Bayano River;* Two Posthumous Works edited by H. Wassén, Gothenburg, 1947

MARDEN, LUIS: *Panama, Bridge of the World*, National Geographic Magazine, Vol. 80, No. 5, 1941

MARSH, R O: *White Indians of Darien*, New York, 1934 (Putnam's, New York)

MILES, WALTER: *Designs for Craftsmen*, Doubleday, Garden City, NY, 1962

NORDENSKIÖLD, ERLAND and WASSÉN, HENRY: *An Historical and Ethnological Survey of the Cuna Indians*, Comparative Ethnographical Studies, Vol. 10, Gothenburg, 1938; *Picture-Writing*, ditto, Vol. 7, 1928

PITTIER, HENRI: *Cuna Indians*, National Geographical Magazine, Vol. 23, No. 7, 1912

SCHIERLING, CHARLOTTE A: *Indianisches Frauentum auf der Weltinsel Amerika*, unpublished but available in the Library of the University of Hamburg, 1971

SEVERIN, TIMOTHY: *The Golden Antilles*, Hamish Hamilton, London, 1970

SEVERIN, TIMOTHY: *Vanishing Primitive Man*, Thames and Hudson, London, 1973

SIEBER, ROY: *African Textiles and Decorative Arts*, The Museum of Modern Art, New York, 1972

STEIN, SIR AUREL: *On Ancient Central Asian Tracks*, MacMillan, London, 1933

STEWARD, J H: *The Circum-Caribbean Tribes*, Bureau of American Ethnology, Bulletin 143, Smithsonian Institution, Washington, DC, 1948

STOUT, DAVID B: *The Cuna*, a Chapter in Handbook of South American Indians, Vol. 4, which is the Steward, J.H Reference.

SYMONDS, MARY and PREECE, LOUISA: *Needlework through the Ages*, Hodder & Stoughton, London, 1928

WAFER, LIONELL: *A New Voyage and Description of the Isthmus of America*, The Hakluyt Society, Edited, Introduction and Notes by L E Elliot Joyce, 1933

WASSÉN, HENRY: *Some Words on the Cuna Indians and Especially their 'Mola' Garments*, Revista do Museu Paulista, NS, Vol. XV

WASSÉN, HENRY: *Contributions to Cuna Ethnography, Result of Expedition to Panama and Colombia 1947*, Etnologiska Studier No. 16, Gothenburg

Books about stitches and techniques

Embroidery Stitches, Barbara Snook, Batsford, London

Mary Thomas's Dictionary of Embroidery Stitches, Hodder and Stoughton, London.

Mary Thomas's Embroidery Book, Hodder and Stoughton, London.

Inspiration for Embroidery, Constance Howard, Batsford, London: Branford, Newton Centre, Massachusetts.

Machine Embroidery: technique and design, Jennifer Gray, Batsford, London: Branford, Newton Centre, Massachusetts.

Design in Embroidery, Kathleen Whyte, Batsford, London: Branford, Newton Centre, Massachusetts.

The Basic Stitches of Embroidery, Ann Victoria Wade, Victoria and Albert Museum publication, 1966

100 Embroidery Stitches, J. & P. Coats, Glasgow.

Index

Appliqué 7, 8, 11, 13, 19, 29, 31, 56, 75–115, 122, 124, 142, 175, 179
Ayrshire embroidery 31

Basket 17, 29, 30, 35, 117, 124
Bayeux Tapestry 8
Bell, Eleanor 120, 121, 129
Berlin woolwork 82
Broderie Anglaise 29, 31, 40–43, 66
Broderie Perse 80
Brown, Lady Richmond 120, 128, 190
Buttonhole 29, 30, 35–37

Canvas work 82
Couching 29, 84, 85, 102, 103, 105
Counterchange 79, 80, 88
Cross 11, 13, 18, 19
Cutwork 7, 11, 13, 28–75, 78, 113, 114, 175

Darning 30, 38, 39, 59, 105
Decoration 7, 8, 24, 27, 29, 31, 34, 40, 47, 77–79, 83, 117, 119, 122
Drawn fabric 52, 53, 58, 60, 63
Drawn thread 30, 31, 44, 45, 59, 62, 63, 65, 67, 69, 71, 81
Dresden work 30, 31
Durchbruch 29

Family cloth (*Familien Tuch*) 31, 69, 71
Fret 18, 19, 99, 143
Fringe 13, 26, 27, 119

Hardanger embroidery 31, 63
Hedebo embroidery 31, 63

Italian cutwork 29, 31, 60

Klosterblock 62
Knotting 30, 82
Kuna 7, 11–15, 19, 22, 23, 80, 82, 91, 108, 116–201, 203

Lace 29, 53–55, 57–59, 63, 66, 69, 73, 91, 103
Lacis (net) 30
Lentencloth (*Hungertuch*) 30

Machine embroidery 66, 102, 113, 115, 123
Madeira work 31
Mask 14, 15, 152, 153, 162
Mola 11, 12, 15, 23, 82, 117–201, 226
Morris, William 81

Needleweaving 53, 60, 63, 64, 67, 69, 111
Net 30, 58, 59, 75, 91
Nordenskiöld 117, 120–122

Openwork 30
Outlining 30, 76, 77, 79
Overcasting 29, 30, 34, 48, 59, 63, 65, 99

Panama 7, 11, 17, 22, 116–118, 120, 121, 123–125
Patch 14, 80, 94, 99, 124, 128, 162–168
Patchwork 77, 79, 80, 82, 95, 99, 120
Picot 31, 53, 63
Picture writing 12, 13, 117, 121, 122, 129–131, 136, 175
Piedrahita, Dr Lucas F.E. 119
Point de Saxe 30
Pulled work 30, 31, 44, 45
Punch work 31
Punto in aria 30, 52–54, 57
Punto tagliato 30
Punto tirato 30

Quilting 24, 30, 56, 76, 77, 79, 80, 95, 96, 98, 99, 175

Raised work 30, 78, 82
Rank 8, 119, 123
Renaissance embroidery 29, 48, 50

Resht work 79
Ribbon appliqué 88
Ribbon embroidery 79
Richelieu work 29, 31
Rickrack 123, 127, 175

Sabrina work 80
Sampler 38, 43–45, 54, 55, 59, 60, 63, 65
Sculpture 11, 13, 29, 47, 52, 79, 82
Shell 12, 20, 78, 212–215
Simple cutwork 29, 49
Slashed work 29, 32–34
Spiral 12, 13, 20, 76, 77, 99, 147, 213
Status 7, 8, 13, 24, 107, 127
Stitches:
    blanket 44, 45, 48, 69, 80
    bullion knots 31, 64
    buttonhole 29, 30, 34, 42, 48–50, 53, 60, 63, 66, 73, 80, 91
    chain 30, 55, 69, 71, 73, 79, 80, 87
    darning 30, 105
    eyelet holes 34, 36, 37, 40, 44–46, 52, 55, 69, 73
    faggot 60
    foursided 31, 60, 71
    french knot 48, 49, 64
    hem 80, 91, 92, 94, 99, 101, 157
    herringbone 80, 105
    knot 30, 55, 69, 71
    looped 29
    overcast 42, 69
    running 42, 95, 99, 127
    satin 48, 49, 53, 60, 63, 66, 69, 111, 113
    stem 42, 48, 63
    surface 30, 31, 34, 37, 44, 45, 55, 63, 64, 114
    whipping 91
Stumpwork 78, 82
Swastika 11, 16
Symbols 7, 8, 10–27, 77, 78, 90, 99, 102, 107, 121–123, 130, 138, 141, 144, 162, 175, 212

Tassel 13
Triangle 12, 101, 176, 178

Umbilical cord 12

Venetian cutwork 29, 75

Wafer, Lionell 118, 119, 121
Wassén, H. 117, 122
Weaving 29, 30, 35, 38, 78, 83,
 119, 123, 124
Wheel (spiderweb) 50, 60, 63, 66
Whipping 29

Y symbol 12, 19, 23, 151

Zigzag line 12, 101, 127, 130, 175,
 176, 178